Patricia H. Hinchey

Finding Freedom
in the Classroom

A Practical Introduction
to Critical Theory

PETER LANG
New York • Washington, D.C./Baltimore • Boston
Bern • Frankfurt am Main • Berlin • Vienna • Paris

Curr
LC
196
H55
1998

Library of Congress Cataloging-in-Publication Data

Hinchey, Patricia H.
Finding freedom in the classroom: a practical introduction
to critical theory / Patricia H. Hinchey.
p. cm. — (Counterpoints; v. 24)
Includes bibliographical references (p.   ) and index.
1. Critical pedagogy. 2. Critical theory. 3. Postmodernism and education.
I. Title. II. Series: Counterpoints (New York, N.Y.); vol. 24.
LC196.H55   370.11'5—dc20   96-23783
ISBN 0-8204-2885-X
ISSN 1058-1634

Die Deutsche Bibliothek-CIP-Einheitsaufnahme

Hinchey, Patricia H.:
Finding freedom in the classroom: a practical introduction to critical theory /
Patricia H. Hinchey. –New York; Washington, D.C./Baltimore; Boston; Bern;
Frankfurt am Main; Berlin; Vienna; Paris: Lang.
(Counterpoints; Vol. 24)
ISBN 0-8204-2885-X
NE: GT

Cover design by James F. Brisson.

The paper in this book meets the guidelines for permanence and durability
of the Committee on Production Guidelines for Book Longevity
of the Council of Library Resources.

© 1998 Peter Lang Publishing, Inc., New York

Printed in the United States of America.

Table of Contents

Preface

Last year, my husband Ed and I planned to drive to a conference in South Carolina, leaving from Pennsylvania after I'd finished teaching my afternoon classes. To save time, he agreed to get food to eat en route. As he left for the office early in the morning, I asked him to pick up my dream lunch: from our favorite deli, I wanted the corned beef sandwich I knew and loved—fragrant meat lavished with mustard, piled inches high on crusty rye bread. As Ed left his office that afternoon, announcing his plans as he left, an office worker reminded him that it was Ash Wednesday, a serious day of fasting for us. The result of the reminder was that after a day spent lustfully anticipating corned beef, I mournfully ended up downing a soggy tuna sandwich that tasted distinctly like catfood on cardboard.

No doubt about it: if you're expecting one thing and get another, you're likely to be dissatisfied with what you get, and that's as true for readers as for eaters. First things first, then: expectations.

If you expect crisp definitions and recipes for classroom activities, you will be disappointed. And you won't find exhaustive analysis and fine distinctions, either. I haven't tried to transform readers into experts on critical theory. Instead, I've simply tried to provide food for thought to nourish readers' thinking about their own classrooms and what happens there.

In effect, I hope this book will help you explore critical theory in the same way that a particular store has helped me explore music. After a childhood soothed by my mother's Mancini and Sinatra, and after teen years reverberating to rock, I became bored with what I was listening to and decided to branch out. This turned out to be easier said than done, though, because I didn't know where to start. How could I know if I would like jazz if I had no experience with it? A dictionary definition—which could tell me *about* jazz but couldn't make me hear it in my imagination—wouldn't help. There were so many choices that I became paralyzed and didn't buy anything. Who wants to invest in something that they might not like later?

Finally, I found a store where I could listen to specific albums marked only with terms like *jazz* and *new age*. By listening to a wide range of individual examples, I started developing a sense of various genres. By listening to several albums in a single category, I started picking up on differences between styles and artists. Now, I buy new age, blues, and some country. I know that I can safely buy anything by Lyle Lovett or Mary Chapin Carpenter, but also that I should probably pass on Garth Brooks. Essentially, the store simply said "There is a category called _____, and here is an album by _____ which is a good exemplar in this category." That skeletal information was all that I needed to explore and to grow, and it is the same kind of information that I hope you find here.

Just as I felt limited in the music I played, many teachers feel limited in what they do in their classrooms. They are tired of old routines and often think "this isn't enough. Something more has to be possible—but what?" The similar reactions aren't surprising, given that many of us learn to teach in much the same way we learn about music. First, we follow the lead of our elders. Then, when we develop some maturity, we try on something new. But even so, our something new comes from a supply of fairly standard choices. Teens normally turn from ballads to rock, not to opera, and teachers are nearly as predictable.

We may stop assigning textbook chapters in order, but we usually keep the textbook. We may start assigning essay tests, but we usually keep the multiple choice sections too. And when we continue to be nagged by a sense that we're still not doing enough, that there's still something important missing from our practice, many of us start looking for new possibilities, but we are overwhelmed and paralyzed in our initial attempts. What do we change, and how do we start when we have no experience with alternatives and are reluctant to just pick something we may not like when we try it out?

I hope this book will be a practical starting point for teachers interested in exploring alternatives for creating a new kind of classroom experience, both for themselves and for their students. Critical theory, an important genre of thinking about school reform, offers most educators an approach to education as radically different from the norm of current practice as new age music is from rock. Just as the music store provided me with a label and a range of examples, each chapter after the first bears a label from critical theory (*epistemology, hegemony, praxis* and so on) and includes several real world examples that relate to that concept. I hope that by sampling the experiences grouped here under various labels, readers will be able to start developing their own sense of the concepts and to see what directions might interest them in the future. To place these discussions in a practical context, the first chapter explores the question of why anyone might see theory as a starting place for change.

There is no attempt to discriminate among various subgroups within the field. With no sense of what jazz is at all, how could anyone follow a debate on the merits of various jazz saxophonists and styles? With no sense of where feminism fits into the big picture of critical theory, how could anyone follow a debate on whose version of feminism is most useful? Again, first things first.

Essentially, this is a book about vision—the critical theorists' vision of a better world through a different kind of education, and your emerging vision of whether and how critical pedagogy might operate in your classroom.

As for my own vision, I am grateful to many who provided nourishing food for thought. I am indebted to all who have shared a classroom with me, on either side of a desk; to all who have conversed with me in person, in their writing, or through their art; and to all who have challenged what I held to be true. For the fact that I know what vision is, and that my own is in focus, I especially thank Jonas Soltis. For the freedom to pursue it, I thank my husband Ed, and children Shawna and E. M., whose patience and support have been boundless. And for the collegiality and invaluable feedback that helped nurture this particular text into print, I thank my writing friends—most especially my tireless cheerleader and clearheaded critic, Melanie Morgon.

ACKNOWLEDGMENTS

The author wishes to thank the publishers and copyright holders for permission to reprint excerpts in this book, as listed below.

Frost, Robert. Mending wall. From *The poetry of Robert Frost*, edited by Edward Connery Lathem. Copyright © 1958 by Robert Frost. Copyright © 1967 by Lesley Frost Ballantine. Copyright 1930, 1939, © 1969 by Henry Holt and Company, Inc. Reprinted by permission of Henry Holt and Company, Inc. and Jonathan Cape.

Walker, Alice. We alone. From *Horses make a landscape look more beautiful* and *Her blue body everything we know*. Copyright © 1984 by Alice Walker, reprinted by permission of Harcourt Brace & Company and The Women's Press, respectively.

Editor's Preface

Patricia Hinchey is one of those special individuals who through a combination of talent, hard work, and commitment have become a treasured teacher. Since she is my colleague in the Penn State system, I periodically encounter a student who has taken one of her classes. "Oh, yeah," they tell me in response to my inquiry concerning their comprehension of a critical concept, "I had Pat Hinchey and I understand all of this." Their next comment usually involves their fondness for her and assessment that she is the best teacher they ever had. The expertise and care that Pat brings to her teaching is evident in this book. As you read it, you will quickly discover what I mean.

Critical theory/critical pedagogy is a difficult area to teach. Much of the time its main concepts are not merely unfamiliar to students but run counter-intuitive to their educational, school-related experiences. Those of us who identify with critical theory and critical pedagogy understand the reality of this disconnection—sometimes we know the pain and anger the attempt to address critical concepts elicits. Pat Hinchey is keenly aware of these dynamics and grounds *Finding Freedom in the Classroom: A Practical Introduction to Critical Theory* on such understandings. Bringing her gifted teaching ability to the pedagogical negotiating table, she provides a smart, experience-based introduction to the field. When I first read the draft of the book, I was struck by the uniqueness of Pat's approach to the topic. In a sense the book is designed for two audiences: (1) Hinchey's intended audience—teacher education and other students who are encountering critical theory for the first time; and (2) those of us who are familiar with the critical discourse. For the first audience the book serves as the best introduction to the field now available. For the second audience the work may be read as an experiment in voice, an effort to take up critical theory from a different lived space. In this context, I believe, the book breaks new ground and adds an exciting new perspective to critical studies.

The difficulty of teaching critical theory and critical pedagogy often moves some introduction-to-the-field authors to simplify the topic in order to make it more palatable to the reader. In this context such reductionism is often accompanied by a depoliticization designed to render critical theory less threatening. Stripped of its complexity and political edge, the critical theory that emerges in such books is an impostor, a pretender that presents critical work as a method of teaching that is more informal, maybe more fun, and more relevant to the concerns of students. This is not critical teaching and it certainly is not what Hinchey presents here. While the book is reader-friendly and sensitive to the reader's background, it does not seek to protect the fragile reader. Hinchey unabashedly takes on the central concepts of critical theory in all their power and controversiality. Indeed, Hinchey is sufficiently true to her subject that she runs the risk of getting into trouble with the wielders of power.

I am proud to introduce Patricia Hinchey's book to the readers of Shirley Steinberg and my Counterpoints Series with Peter Lang Publishers. Few books capture the spirit of the series as much as *Finding Freedom in the Classroom: A Practical Introduction to Critical Theory*. This book will make waves and leave the field better off as a result of the disturbance. We extend a sincere thanks to Lang publisher Chris Myers for his support of Counterpoints and books such as this.

Joe L. Kincheloe
Penn State University

Chapter One

WHO CARES?
Why Theory—and Critical Theory in Particular—Matters

Before I built a wall I'd ask to know
What I was walling in or walling out
Robert Frost

THE WAY THINGS *ARE*

When I taught literature courses for undergraduates, I asked a habitual question: "How many people are in a marriage, and what sex are they?" My students had an equally habitual response: "*WHAT?*" I had to ask the question at least three times and then discuss Mormons and Muslims before they could begin to comprehend it.

But then, why should my students have responded with anything but bewilderment? We learn from our experience, and daily life in America teaches that marriage occurs between heterosexual pairs. If we hear about alternatives, it's usually in a rare media blitz when a gay couple loses custody of a child or sues for equal rights. And, in those cases, the media attention itself signals that something out of the ordinary, something we wouldn't expect, is going on. My students had never questioned the number and sex of people in a marriage because the formula was self-evident in their own families and neighborhoods, in what they read, and in what they saw on television and billboards. Marriages contain one man and one woman. Period. The world they inhabit told them so, implicitly if not explicitly.

Most people have much the same reaction when asked about various practices in schools: "Why use textbooks? Why have standardized tests? Why divide work into discrete academic subjects? Why spend so much time inside school and so little outside it?" . . . "WHAT?" Just as we learn what marriage is from everyday life, we learn what school is from our experiences there. Researchers have shown that our ideas about school are as deeply ingrained as my students' ideas about marriage. "Not use textbooks? Not have tests? Not have subjects? Inconceivable." Such unquestioning acceptance of current practice permeates schooling.

Once, for example, I investigated how a group of student teachers thought about and handled homework in their classes. Most reported feeling like a "real teacher" when they gave their classes homework assignments, but few could explain exactly why they made the assignments or exactly what purpose the work would serve. In fact, their responses often took the *WHAT?* form: "What do you mean, *why* did I give homework? That's what teachers *do!*" In their minds, the actions of a "real teacher" were prescripted, predetermined by some invisible and all-knowing director. Their job was only to play the role as it had already been defined: "One man marries one woman. Teachers give homework. That's just the way it *is*."

DIVINE DECREE . . . OR CULTURAL HABIT?

No matter how strongly we may feel that the way we do things just obviously *is* the way to do them, the truth is that most of what we do is convention . . . habit . . . custom. What we *do* usually has its roots in what we *believe*, and beliefs are not the unshakable foundation for action we usually assume.

For example, some people say that marriage must include a heterosexual pair because they believe that God has dictated that rule and no human can change divine law. But no matter how firmly some may hold this belief, others believe equally firmly that God has endorsed polygamy. Thus, one person's divine truth is another's heresy: who can indisputably lay claim to the definitive "truth" here? Yet it is precisely such deeply held beliefs that permeate our thinking and fuel our actions in countless areas and ways. The firmer our convictions, the more likely we are to feel self-righteous about what we do and to remain oblivious to the fact that others hold very different beliefs and endorse very different customs. The result, far too often, is that conflicting beliefs ignite religious, political, and cultural wars. History is rife with examples ranging from the Romans and the Christians to the Bosnian nightmare of "ethnic cleansing."

Such wars occur because when we are immersed in our family, our religion, our culture, we come to believe that various ideas are unquestionably true. We fail to see that many ideas are only theories about the heavens and the earth rather than a dependable blueprint. Like my students, we absorb cultural *beliefs* and confuse them with *facts*:

1. God says one man, one woman per marriage.
2. People can own land. (And, earlier in our history, even other people.)
3. Hard work will lead to prosperity.

In America, to challenge such statements is the cultural equivalent of religious heresy:

1. Maybe we should legalize homosexual marriages.
2. Maybe the Native Americans had a point about communal caretaking.
3. Maybe all of the poor aren't poor because they're lazy.

Most often, those steeped in mainstream American culture can respond to such contrasting suggestions only with an uncomprehending "WHAT?"

School culture, like all others, is permeated with beliefs and assumptions often mistaken for fact. We talk in terms of who is right and who is wrong, rather than in terms of different views. We forget that the definition of appropriate school practice, like the definition of marriage, depends upon who is doing the defining and when and where they're doing it. We also forget that the definition will be shaped by the assumptions it is based on.

In the early years of the twentieth century, for example, women signed teaching contracts designed by men, who always had authority over schools. Contracts commonly dictated specific tasks the women would do in addition to teaching, including scrubbing the classroom floor weekly. Contracts also commonly imposed specific restrictions on personal matters, including the teacher's social life as well as her clothing. Men decided which other men a teacher might walk or ride with, and when and where she might travel; they specified that teachers wear a minimum of two petticoats, and they banned brightly colored clothes.

Through such detailed contracts, men defined what it meant to be a teacher. Women accepted these definitions and restrictions without challenge because of a prevailing cultural belief that women were weaker creatures than men, who therefore had a natural right to power over them. Now, of course, that belief has been challenged for many years, and it has less public credibility than it once did. Today, when belief in the right of individuals to make their own choices about such matters as clothing is much stronger than it once was, most women teachers would reject such personal restrictions not only from employers, but from their life-partners as well.

Yet however ludicrous a 1920 teaching contract may look to us today, it was "obvious" to most people in the early years of the century that such personal restrictions on women rightfully belonged in the definition of a teacher's responsibilities. It is interesting to speculate on which parts of current practice will look ludicrous to educators a century from now. Representatives of today's mainstream education establishment may talk about what schools "obviously" must do and be, but the reality is that they are no more omniscient than their predecessors who "knew" that teachers "had" to wear two petticoats. However firmly many people may believe their own assertions about schools, those assertions are frequently based upon cultural beliefs that they have absorbed unconsciously—and that they often confuse with fact. Things have been as they are for so long that we rarely stop to talk about the historical rationale for current routines.

For example, for decades schools have embodied many ideas assumed to be self-evident and unquestionably true:

1. Students must be bribed or coerced to learn.
2. Learning is difficult.
3. School must be based on the teaching of subjects.
4. Teachers and administrators know what is best and appropriate for students to study.

Challenging such ideas in many American schools remains the equivalent of educational heresy:

1. Learning is a natural and enjoyable human activity.
2. Learning must be based on personal experience.
3. Students' interests and needs must drive their educational experience.

To many of today's educators, such ideas will seem as unorthodox as the idea that a school director might forbid a teacher to leave town without his permission. And yet, like the earlier ideas which gave way, they are *ideas* rather than *facts*. When we refuse to contemplate contrasting ideas seriously, when we insist that current debates are about *right* and *wrong* rather than competing views and definitions of education, we cultivate the kind of cultural bigotry that has led to war throughout history. Indeed, we see the result of educational bigotry in the bloody battles currently raging over whole language vs. traditional reading instruction. These two camps have very different definitions of "reading" and very different assumptions about what *education* involves. But unfortunately, "debate" between members of each camp often amounts to simplistic verbal sniping.

Like religious zealots, we educators often wreak extensive havoc when we confuse what we *believe* with what we *know*.

UNCOVERING CHOICES

Confusing fact with belief, we also confuse what *is* with what *must be*. If we believe that God has stipulated heterosexual marriages, then we *must* endorse only heterosexual marriages. If we believe that students will not be naturally inclined to learn, then we *must* have extrinsic systems of reward and punishment. Our beliefs guide our actions in every realm of human activity, and when we confuse belief and fact, we stop seeing the countless areas of daily life where we might in fact chart a different course.

That is, we rarely see that our customs constitute one choice among many choices. Immersed in our own culture, we think in terms of doing things the one *right* way rather than in terms of doing things in one of many possible ways. But often there are other things we might do, other choices we might make—if we weren't far more in the grip of habit than we are aware. A psychologist once told me that many of his clients reported having a life-changing revelation when he offered some simple advice: he suggested that they stop answering their phones if they didn't want to be interrupted while doing something. "Not answer my phone?" client after client responded. "How could I do that?" His fantastic answer: "Don't pick it up." For many (and I confess to being one), this was a stunning, liberating, and entirely new possibility. We are creatures of habit indeed. We learn our habits, as we absorb our beliefs, from experience. Unfortunately, we rarely stop to discriminate between the kinds of lessons experience offers. Sometimes, as when we watch a pot boil on the stove, experience does teach us facts; it does teach us about unalterable laws of nature. But other times, as when we go to a wedding and see a bride and a groom, it teaches us how things are commonly done in one culture. There is an enormous difference between custom and natural law, and we create mental cages and inflexible rules when we don't make the kinds of distinctions between *belief* and *fact* outlined earlier. Restrictions imposed by facts may be inflexible, but those imposed by beliefs are not.

We can't stop water from boiling when it reaches a certain temperature, but we *can* stop answering the phone simply because it rings. No matter how compelled we may feel to answer it, the reality is we do not have to. If we stop and take a good hard look at why we do many of the things we've always assumed we have to do, we can uncover options we'd never considered before. As I was writing this chapter, I heard a story that seems to demonstrate the power of habit, of doing what we've always done. What else but a lifelong unquestioned habit of self-sacrifice can possibly explain the sight of a ninety-year-old mother shoveling three feet of snow from around her healthy sixty-year-old son's car? I can almost hear the mother's answer to a question about why she would do such work: "Why? What do you mean *why*? My son's car is buried in snow—That's why I have to shovel it out!" The possibility that her son might take care of his own dratted car didn't seem to occur to her. (And here you see in operation my own habitual assumptions about the proper roles of a mother and son!)

Confusing custom with immutable law is the mistake my students made when they equated the common American definition of marriage with what a marriage *is,* in some unalterable way. They couldn't understand my question about the number and sex of people in a marriage because it never occurred to them that the definition they held wasn't the only one that was possible at all times and places for everyone.

This is the same mistake many make in thinking about educational practice. While it may seem inconceivable not to have textbooks in a classroom, the reality is that we choose to have them. And, we currently choose to have them largely because schools have had them for as long as anyone can remember. Similarly, however much we may feel that homework is as inevitable as the sun rising in the morning, the reality is that assigning nightly homework is one of countless practices we certainly have the power to change. We choose, for example, to have a fragmented secondary schedule of forty-some minutes per class, some eight periods per day. We choose to conduct educational practice primarily in classrooms. We choose to have subjects. We choose to have tests.

Confusing *what is* with *what must be*, we don't recognize that common practices came not from divine decree, but from choices made sometime, somewhere, by someone who *might* have chosen to do otherwise. We lose the ability to imagine a different way of doing things, and the result is a kind of mental paralysis: *WHAT?* The mere suggestion that things could be otherwise stops us dead in our mental tracks, as it did the student teachers I worked with: "What do you mean, *why* did I assign homework? This is *school*; there *has* to be homework."

Unable to imagine alternatives to common habits, we can't weigh the pros and cons of various possibilities and make conscious choices among them. In my literature classes, students couldn't think about the pros and cons of a man having one wife or multiple wives because they simply didn't imagine that any man *could* have multiple wives. They endorsed monogamy because it was endorsed by the culture they lived in, not because of personal conviction or conscious choice. For them, to ask how and why monogamy might be preferable to polygamy made as much sense as asking whether it's a good or bad thing that water boils: that's just the way things *are*. However, if the same students had been born and had grown up in certain parts of Africa, where Muslim men can and do take more than one wife, they would have just as unconsciously assumed polygamy to be the "way things *are*" and might have been equally unable to imagine monogamy.

This paralysis of mind, which limits our imagination, leads to a paralysis of habit that compels some people to answer a ringing phone even when they don't want to. When someone points out they *don't* actually *have* to, they may well stop picking up the phone, feeling much more in control of their own lives, and much happier as well. We can't make choices for ourselves if we don't see places where we could choose to do things differently than we've always done them.

Since many of our unquestioned habits come from choices far-removed from us in time and place, there's a frightening implication of unquestioned endorsement of the status quo, of an acceptance of the way things *are* as the way they *have* to be. The practical reality is that when we fail to recognize and make our own choices, we allow others to make them for us.

LIVING OUT OTHERS' CHOICES

When we do what we've always done out of unquestioned habit, what we're actually doing is operating on a blueprint designed by someone else. When we answer a ringing telephone and allow it to interrupt an important activity, we let someone else's priorities outrank our own: "Somebody wants to talk to me, so I have to make myself available, even though I'm busy." We allow someone else's agenda to usurp our own. Mindlessly, we follow a plan designed by someone else, contributing to whatever it is they intend, ignoring the fact that our own wishes might be different.

The student teachers who assigned homework without knowing why provide a larger case in point. In fact, and somewhere in time, teachers started assigning homework for many reasons. Some wanted to keep students from having free time to get into trouble. Others wanted to promote interaction between parents and children, or wanted students to learn to work independently, or to promote a number of other purposes. Such varied goals, however, are best served by very different kinds of assignments. If the goal is simply to keep students busy, then any work sure to be time-consuming is suitable. But if the goal is to involve parents, then the assignment should require parental interaction, like an interview of some kind. If the goal is to learn to work independently, then the assignment should make it difficult for someone else to help, or include a remote deadline so that the student has to practice self-discipline to get the work done on time.

Because they didn't understand homework as a choice made to serve certain goals, the student teachers soon confronted a practical classroom dilemma: students simply refused to do homework. Day after day, assignments went undone and the student teachers in a single wailing, despairing voice asked me "Why? *Why* won't students do our assignments?" I responded, "Why *should* they do your assignments?" and got the familiar monosyllable: "*WHAT?*" For them, the mere fact that homework was assigned by a teacher was sufficient justification for students to do it. Everyone knows that teachers give homework and students do it. That's just the way it *is*!

But that's not the way it was, and in fact it wasn't very difficult to explain what was happening. Because the student teachers themselves never thought about a rationale for giving homework (except that it's what teachers do), their assignments were not consciously designed to match a clear purpose. In fact, the assignments were usually very bad ones—too hard or too easy for various students, boring in almost every case—mindless and pointless. One student teacher noted in her journal, "I was bored making up a worksheet and they were just as bored doing it. I think that's a problem with homework—it's real busy work, vocabulary and definitions." Again divine decree seems at work, specifying that homework *will* be boring; it's just an inherited fact, something it is not in the teacher's power to change. Readings, too, were assigned willy-nilly (or because they came next in the textbook), and never mind the students' interests and reading abilities.

In fact, the student teachers' classroom practice had much in common with the cooking practice of a wife featured in an anecdote I've heard repeatedly: Watching his wife cook a roast one day, a man asked why she always cut a slice off each end before putting it in a pan. "Well," the wife answered, "my mother always did, but I'm not sure why. I'll ask her." And the mother's reply? "I always cut the ends off my roasts because I never had a pan big enough for them." Doing as others have always done without asking *why* they have done so is no less foolhardy for teachers than for cooks.

In cases like these, the habits are nonproductive, sometimes causing needless work (as in the wife's case), sometimes causing mental disturbance (as in antagonism between young teachers and their students). But the results of acting on someone else's plan, contributing to someone else's purposes and goals, can be much more insidious than this.

CHOICES AS A REFLECTION OF VALUES

Ultimately, everything we do sends a signal about what we value, what we think is important—whether we're aware of the signal we're sending or not. The mother shoveling snow from her son's car signals that she values her son's comfort and convenience more than her own. The doctor who makes a point of being on time for appointments signals that she considers her patients' time as important as her own. The father who reads to his young child daily signals that he values reading as a part of everyday life. Like every other setting, classrooms overflow with value-laden actions.

The homework example offers a demonstration. When a teacher assigns busywork as homework, work that offers students no real benefit but that ties up their after-school time, the assignment embodies several possible signals about what the teacher believes and values. An activity as routine and simple as this might suggest that:

1. Students must be controlled continuously, and/or
2. Teachers are at least partly responsible for controlling students' behavior during after-school hours, and/or
3. Students are better off doing pointless work assigned by a teacher than they would be doing anything they themselves might choose to do in after-school hours, and/or
4. It is sensible to give students with various levels of expertise the same work to do independently, and/or
5. Being busy is important in and of itself.

I don't mean to suggest that the teacher is conscious of sending such signals or endorsing such beliefs, but the action of assigning busywork nevertheless endorses them tacitly. In fact, the most worrisome aspect here is that teachers' actions may promote agendas they would *not* support consciously.

The homework example demonstrates such irony. Many teachers are currently protesting that society expects too much of them; they argue forcefully that they can't and won't take on the responsibilities of parents and social workers. Many would scorn the idea that it's their job to control students after as well as during school. And yet, a teacher who assigns homework that serves no purpose except to keep the students busy is in fact playing the role of an after-school monitor. Let's keep those students busy at night—never mind busy doing what.

This is not a phenomenon confined to areas where youth crime is a concern; it's a perspective that permeates schooling. My children's private college preparatory school offers plenty of evidence. For example, when I asked my daughter's ninth-grade English teacher if the poor girl *really* had to do still more grammar worksheets for homework (after passing a rigorous grammar exam to get into this selective school), the teacher replied that there was "no way" to individualize instruction in her classroom, and that even if my daughter *did* already know the material, doing it again "wouldn't hurt."　I suppose that keeping students bent over paperwork for hours every night is thought (if anyone stopped to think about it) not only to keep them out of trouble, but also to reassure parents that their tuition or tax money has been well spent, that their children are indeed learning. But having watched my daughter being busy for hours without learning a single thing, instead I sympathized with her resentment of the teacher who squandered her precious after-school hours. I also shared her anger over the teacher's implied assumption that my daughter's time wasn't valuable and so could be wasted without a second thought.

Moreover, I disagree with the teacher's assertion that such rote work "doesn't hurt." I taught English long enough to know how bitterly students come to hate a subject when they're forced to do work they mastered in early grades year after year after year. My daughter's case also suggests stupidity in the idea that it's universally sensible to assign the same work to every student in the class. (And again let me admit how much some of my own assumptions and beliefs are reflected in my assertions here.) Some of her classmates had performed poorly on a diagnostic test, but my daughter didn't.

What doctor would prescribe an antibiotic for a patient with an infection—and also for a patient without one? How is it that such wasteful practice is commonly accepted routine in classrooms nationwide? What should students think of teachers who waste their time and who value the appearance of learning over learning itself？ What do pointless school activities teach students about the value of schooling, the value of doing as the teacher says? What do such activities teach students about how much the school culture values them as unique human beings?

And this is but a minor example of the kind of signals our actions send about the beliefs and values operating in school routines. The effect of what we do in classrooms reaches far beyond how students feel about a particular subject and far beyond how they spend their weeknights as teenagers. As if the consequences already outlined aren't serious enough to persuade us to think more carefully about what we do in classrooms, there are even larger consequences to consider.

THE BIG PICTURE OF SCHOOLING

Students are immersed in school culture in the same way all of us are immersed in our national culture. Their experiences in schools promote beliefs in the same way that all cultural experiences promote beliefs. A man and a woman in every marriage teaches us that heterosexual monogamy is the norm. Seeing textbooks in every school teaches us that every school has subjects and textbooks.

However, the lessons that schooling teaches students range far beyond academic ones. Schools have always had other purposes. Public schools are funded with taxpayer money for a good reason: public schools are designed to serve the interests of the state. Yes, of course we want children to be able to read and write and we talk a great deal about equal opportunity, but there are reasons for supporting public schools that are not in the least altruistic.

We want citizens who can read and write—and so vote, and so feel they are an active part of government, and so support democracy (and not work to undermine it). We want citizens who can read and write—and so be gainfully employed and not dependent on the state, and so become contributors to the national economy. We want citizens who follow rules and have respect for authority, and so pay their taxes conscientiously and obey laws. And so on, and so on, and so on. There are now and always have been social, political, and economic purposes for the establishment of schools, public schools in particular.

Today's public schools have grown out of the common school movement of the early 1800s, based on the idea that a common education for all children would benefit society in several ways. At a time when immigrants from varied countries were flooding the United States, it was thought that if children from different social, ethnic, and religious backgrounds attended the same school and interacted on a daily basis, then friction among various groups who must coexist peacefully in this democracy would be reduced. If children learned skills and habits that made them desirable in the workplace, then poverty and its constant companion, crime, would also be reduced. If all children learned to think of democracy as the best political system and to value patriotism, then the government could depend on the support of its citizens and not worry about internal rebellion. A major task of public schools has always been to produce citizens with a common core of knowledge who think of themselves as patriotic Americans and who can be financially independent of the state.

It is for these very practical reasons—and not an altruistic interest in social justice—that schools have received state support. (Anyone who doubts this might look at the recent history of New Jersey, where voters nearly impeached a governor who tried to change school funding so that poor children would receive an education comparable to that of children from wealthier communities. The governor wasn't impeached, but his reforms were repealed, and he lost the next election.) Common school practices now considered a necessary part of schooling were, in fact, chosen to help create a compliant and patriotic populace.

The ideal of America as the great melting pot, where varied ethnicities would meld together to form "the American citizen," accounts for the fact that schools nationwide have a common curriculum, and also for the fact that the common curriculum is Eurocentric and male-dominated. The early goal of preparing docile and tireless workers for America's growing factories does much to explain why so much of school is repetitious and boring, stressing hard work and doing as one is told, over and over, without question.

It didn't have to be this way. Children of Irish immigrant families might have learned more about the history of the Irish in America and less about William Penn. They might have learned more about Sybil Ludington's

1777 ride to assemble her father's regiment to defend Danbury from the British—and less about Betsy Ross's sewing skills. They might have read Sojourner Truth's moving feminist speeches as well as Benjamin Franklin's maxims. Children might have been encouraged, rather than discouraged, from asking questions about why they have to take tests and why they always read history texts and rarely contemporary literature. But these choices might have led to different mindsets on the part of the students—and the melting pot agenda and the factory agenda were well-established at the time.

Because we are so far removed in time and place from these beginnings, few teachers would recognize themselves as acting in service to these agendas. In fact, many would strenuously oppose the idea that their work with children is designed to nurture robot-like work habits suitable only for routine and poorly paid jobs. Nevertheless, continued acceptance of many practices that constitute "the way things are" equates to tacit endorsement of those goals. It doesn't matter, for example, that my daughter's teacher probably didn't mean to signal that schoolwork will often be useless. When she assigned a useless task, that message was unavoidably embodied in her action, no matter what she intended. She also implicitly endorsed the idea that people should accept without question and accustom themselves to mind-numbing routines (a habit that might have stood me in good stead the summer during my college career when I worked swing shift at a factory and found myself peering over a light table looking for cracks in glass bottles at 3 a.m.).

For many, this connection between following an unquestioned classroom routine and promoting the current social, political, and economic status quo will seem a leap as large as that from the north to the south rim of the Grand Canyon. Certainly, if pursued to its logical conclusion, this line of thinking is equally dangerous—from the perspective of those who *enjoy* the status quo. But no matter how firmly we have been taught to believe that schools operate in the best interests of students and as a means of opportunity for them, the reality is that much of what we do is based not on ideals of equal opportunity, but on a far different agenda.

THE USEFULNESS OF CRITICAL THEORY

In a Zen parable, a young fish asks an elder fish to define the nature of the sea. The young one complains that although everyone talks constantly about the sea, he can't see it and he can't really get a clear understanding of what it is. The wise elder notes that the sea is all around the young one; it is where he was born and where he will die; it is a sort of envelope, and he can't see it because he is part of it.

Such is the difficulty of coming to understand our own cultural beliefs and how they influence our actions. Like the fish who has trouble understanding the very sea surrounding him, we have trouble identifying the influence of our culture because we are immersed in it and are part of it; we have been since birth and we will be until death—or until an experience with a different culture shows us that things might be other than the way we've always known them to be.

It is in overcoming this difficulty that critical theory is especially valuable. It offers us a new perspective to use in analyzing our experiences, as the fish would get an entirely new perspective on the sea if he were able to consider it from a beach. The lens of critical theory refocuses our vision of the place we've lived all our lives. As is true of all theory (Maybe man can learn to fly. Maybe the sun doesn't revolve around the earth.), the usefulness of critical theory is that it helps open our minds to possibilities we once found unimaginable. (Maybe standardized tests aren't reliable. Maybe tracking promotes inequality rather than equality.) Once such heresies are imagined, we can explore them. And maybe in our explorations, as in the explorations of other revolutionaries, we can change the face of the way things *are,* forever.

Critical theory is about possibility, and hope, and change. It calls our attention to places where choices have been made, and it clarifies whose goals those choices have served. It calls our attention to the fact that we might have chosen otherwise. Indeed, it proposes a radically different vision of schooling and urges us to make different choices. Whether you accept these revolutionary goals is for you to decide. But whatever your decision, exploring the world of critical theory means that you will forever see far more freedom in your classroom than you once imagined possible.

Chapter Two

UNPACKING "THE WAY IT IS"
Constructed Consciousness and Hegemony

Adults, older girls, shops, magazines, newspapers, window signs—all the world had agreed that a blue-eyed, pink-skinned doll was what every girl treasured. "Here," they said, "this is beautiful, and if you are on this day 'worthy' you may have it."

Toni Morrison

VALUES AS A BASIS FOR ACTION

Critical theory is, above all else, a way to ask questions about power. Who has it? How did they get it? How do they keep it? What are they doing with it? How do their actions affect the less powerful? How might things be otherwise?

We tend to think of the world as a place where things just happen, as a place that somehow arranges itself, one where our own actions make little or no difference in the big picture. But we're wrong. Somewhere, somehow, someone does something, and something else happens as a result. Two cars collide not unavoidably, but because their drivers made choices. Each driver chose to take one route rather than another. Either might have taken a few seconds more or less to get into the car. Either might have stopped for gas. Both might have stayed home. Any change in their actions would very likely have changed the consequences.

The reality that different choices lead to different outcomes, that people actually trigger events (either consciously or unconsciously), is evident on a much larger scale as well. *Some*one writes legislation, someone else votes on it, and still others gain or lose privilege or pay more or less taxes. *Some*one writes policy manuals, someone endorses the policy, and as a result someone else has fewer or more vacation days, or gets more or less notice before being fired. *Some*one writes textbooks, and *some*one publishes them, and *some*one buys them. And, as a result, teachers teach one curriculum rather than another, and children learn that certain people are important and others are not.

Critical theory looks at how the choices of one group affect the lives of others and asks: Who are these *some*ones who make the decisions that yield such important consequences for others? How did these *some*ones come to be the decision makers who have so much power? From the perspective of the critical theorist, the key to such questions often lies in cultural values. If one group holds power over another, it is often because the culture has taught members of the less powerful group to accept a value system that bestows privilege on others.

A simple example comes from my daily life. Although it doesn't demonstrate fully the kind of situations that concern critical theorists (and which I will detail momentarily), this example does illustrate how our values lead to deference to others: I have an elderly aunt and uncle who have been good to me all my life and who make somewhat imperious and often inconvenient requests of my family members. Because of our values, each of us shovels snow or runs ten miles to the grocery store for a single item without hesitation. We value my aunt and uncle's past and present kindness and generosity; we value close bonds with family members; we respect the elderly and believe it fair to help those who cared for us when we were young. Holding these values, we agree to let their desires take precedence over our own convenience; we do what they say, however inconvenient, rather than what we want.

This is a conscious decision my husband and I have made; it reflects values that we know we hold and that we have taught explicitly to our children. The fact that we are conscious of our values and the link between them and our actions is what sets this example apart from the concerns of the critical theorist. Rather than instances of conscious choice and action, the critical theorist seeks to uncover situations in which one group *unquestioningly* and/or *unconsciously* accepts a value system that results in privilege for some other group at the cost of its own welfare. That is, group members defer to others without having thought critically about the values influencing their actions.

An obvious example here is the experience of children, who as a group generally have little power. Indeed, their family and culture is likely to teach them from birth that a "good" child respects and obeys adults. So ingrained is this belief in children that a child who wants to be judged "good" may submit to repeated sexual abuse because she believes that what adults want is always more important than her own feelings and physical welfare. Children are explicitly taught *not* to question what adults tell them, and they generally accept unquestioning obedience as a value long before they are capable of thinking critically about consequences. Adults, too, can accept the values of others unquestioningly, in a childlike way. When they do, they give others the right to make decisions and to dictate actions, no matter whom those decisions and actions benefit or hurt.

For example, an employee in the tobacco industry might cooperate with an unethical policy because he believes that he has no right to question his superiors in management. Or, a student might not challenge a professor over an essay that received a poor grade because she believes that professors are always right. Or, a welfare recipient might endure rude treatment from bureaucrats without protest, believing that anyone who can't earn a living can't expect respect. In such situations, there is an acceptance, often unconscious, of values and judgments that result in some people being slotted into superior, and others inferior, roles.

The critical theorist calls this passive acceptance of value judgments that privilege others constructed consciousness, which is said to be operating whenever one group adopts a set of values or ideas that places it at a disadvantage.[1] Constructed consciousness is evident in the following ideas because embedded in each is acceptance of inferior status based on roles: "I agree that good employees don't question their superiors. I agree that all professors are smarter than all students. I agree that poor people are probably lazy and don't deserve respect." Whether we endorse these ideas consciously or not, when we believe we have no right to challenge the supervisor/professor/bureaucrat, our action signals that we are willing to grant superiority based on who has which job, who is on which side of a desk, or who has more money.

In such situations, the critical theorist says that the more powerful group has attained hegemony over the less powerful. When hegemony is operating, the less powerful do as they're told and accept the inferior roles assigned to them without question. Individual merit and the right of every human being to be treated with respect are ignored; the value of a human being becomes confused with his job and bank account. Constructed consciousness allows inequity to go unexamined and unchecked—in virtually every facet of daily life.

"THAT'S NO LADY, THAT'S MY WIFE"

The experience of women is just one area that demonstrates how one group (women) has accepted a value system that grants another group (men) dominance over them. (For this reason, much writing in the field of critical theory involves feminism.) In American culture, as in many others, men have long held hegemony over women, have long held the position of decision makers who shape events. My own experience overflows with relevant anecdotes; one of the most striking occurred years ago.

As a newly minted professional, I had a conversation with a colleague approaching retirement, and our talk has stayed with me for over a decade. We were sitting over a breakfast of coffee and rolls, and I was asking about her plans when she left teaching. "Well," she responded. "That would depend on whether Lou decides he wants to marry me." "Is that what *you* want then?" I asked, "to marry Lou?" "Well I don't know," she replied. "If he wants to marry me, then I'll marry him. If he doesn't want to marry me, then I won't be getting married. It's up to him."

Up to *him*? I thought. Well, yes, of course, his thoughts on the subject would matter, but shouldn't *she* also be making some independent decision about what *she* wanted? No matter what tack I took in trying to draw out her own feelings and thoughts, though, she came back repeatedly to a scenario in which decisions about the future lay entirely in Lou's hands. She never said anything like, "Well, he's grand and I love him madly. I think he'd be a terrific husband and a great companion for my retirement years." Not at all. Just "Whatever he wants is what will happen." (What happened, by the way, is that they became unofficially "engaged." Then, he strung her along for a few more years, until his funeral, where she met another woman who was also "engaged" to Lou and who had waited equally long for him to decide he was ready to take a bride.)

I remember the conversation so clearly because I was stunned at the time that anyone could be so passive about a life choice as significant as marriage. I remember being amazed that this woman seemed unable to imagine having a voice that mattered on the issue. She was smart. She was attractive. She had an independent income. How was it that she saw herself in terms of goods on a shelf waiting for a shopper to take notice?

Here again is the critical theorist's question: how does it happen that some people, like this woman, devalue themselves and elevate others? And again in this case, the answer is that people act against their own interest because of constructed consciousness: they accept a value system that demeans their own worth. In this case, the woman's culture sent her signals from birth that her opinions, her desires, her thinking, her very life had less value than that of any man, and so she came to accept the idea that men were stronger, smarter—more valuable—than she. Her religion, which (like many others) has a long tradition of wives submitting to their husbands' will, reinforced the messages in television shows and on billboards. Didn't Lucy need Desi to get her out of scrapes (which she never would have gotten into in the first place if she'd listened to him)? Didn't Father know best? Wasn't her own Father to be obeyed without question? Wasn't her Department Chair a man, her Dean a man, her Chief Executive Officer a man? Weren't her advisors for her doctorate men? Everywhere in her experience were men with power, and women without it, to teach her the lesson that men matter and women don't. Everywhere were lessons to teach her that a "good" woman pleases the men in her life rather than herself.

Schools, in fact, have offered explicit lessons on the supporting role women "ought" to play. Here, for example, is a passage from a 1950s home economics text, taken from a section titled "How To Be a Good Wife." (Though more than one colleague has given me copies of this passage, none of us has been able to track down the specific source.)

Have dinner ready. Plan ahead, even the night before, to have a delicious meal on the table. This is a way of letting him know that you have been thinking about him and are concerned about his needs. Most men are hungry when they come home and the prospect of a good meal is part of the warm welcome needed.

Prepare yourself. Take fifteen minutes to rest so that you will be refreshed when he arrives. Touch up your make-up, put a ribbon in your hair and be fresh looking. He has been with a lot of work weary people. Be a little gay and a little more interesting. His boring day may need a lift.

Prepare the children. Take a few minutes to wash the children's hands and faces (if they are small), comb their hair, and if necessary change their clothes. They are little treasures and he would like to see them playing the part.

Make him comfortable. Have him lean back in a comfortable chair or suggest that he lie down in the bedroom. Have a cool or warm drink ready for him. Arrange his pillow and offer to take off his shoes. Speak in a low, soft, soothing and pleasant voice. Allow him to relax and unwind. Listen to him. You may have a dozen things to tell him, but the moment of his arrival is not the time. Let him talk first.

Make the evening his. Never complain if he does not take you out to dinner or to other pleasant entertainment. Instead, try to understand his world of strain and pressure, his need to unwind and relax.

No wonder that women a short generation or so ahead of me continued to defer to the idea that men have some inalienable right to make decisions for the pretty little ladies.

Sadly, experience has taught me that a willingness to yield to male supremacy is still common among the generations that followed. I've encountered woman after woman my own age and younger who allow men to order their lives, endorsing the idea that men are more important and know more than women. Some drive only the car their husbands select, even if they make their own car payments. Some can't go away without their husband's permission. Some serve what their husbands order for dinner at a time their husbands specify, no matter what else they might have done that day.

One of my friends reports having a mental earthquake when a psychologist asked her *why* she had to do all the things she was complaining about doing. "Oh," she instantly replied, knowing well the catastrophic consequences of doing otherwise: "John will get mad if I don't." *"So?"* the psychologist queried. *"SO??"* my friend responded, incredulous that the tragedy wasn't self-evident. For her, the possibility that the sun would rise and the birds would sing every morning *even if* her husband were angry was so radical that it shook the very foundations of her world view. Another friend, in the middle of a hostile divorce, drove a weekly round trip, taking nearly four hours in an unreliable car that often broke down, so that her estranged husband could visit a few hours with their young daughter. "Why do you do all the driving?" I asked. Her response? "Mark told me to."

Lou, John, Mark: decision makers. And the women attached to them? Insignificant. Their duty was to do as they were told, to please the men. The women themselves agreed that their own wishes were irrelevant when a man stood next to them with demands. Men matter; women don't.

While these examples may seem obvious and extreme to many of us, to the women holding such mindsets, the idea that they did not have to live as others dictated was beyond imagining. However incomprehensible such passivity may seem to others, a similar lack of imagination and lack of self-worth is common among widely varied groups. While women continue to live with men who abuse them, many men accept abuse from women. Many of the elderly accept abuse from their grown children and grandchildren. Many workers live in constant terror of a whimsical and mean-spirited supervisor.

Somewhere, somehow, someone or something has taught large numbers of people to accept powerlessness and discrimination. Many people have learned that they are deficient in some way; that they are unimportant; that they aren't worthy of being treated well; that they deserve no better than they get. Unfortunately, it is much easier to see constructed consciousness and hegemony at work in the lives of others. Most teachers, for example, would be stunned by the idea that they *allow* others to have power over them, just as my friends were stunned by the idea that they *could* say "No!" to the men who were telling them what to do. Still, no matter how hard it may be for teachers to imagine, the reality is that they are one of many groups who frequently cooperate in their own oppression by uncritically accepting ideas that permeate their culture.

THAT'S NO LADY, THAT'S A TEACHER

One sentence that I hear repeatedly from teachers pierces my body like the screech of fingernails on a blackboard. I ask, "What do you teach?" and a teacher invariably responds "Oh, I *only* teach elementary school," or "I'm *only* a first [or second or fourth] grade teacher." Only?

Teachers determine whether children find learning exciting or dull, whether they find it an enjoyable natural activity or a difficult and intimidating one. Teachers introduce children to the magic of the written word, to the wondrous mental adventures books provide, and to the satisfying logic of math. Teachers teach children that adults can be trusted—or not; that everyone ought to treat everyone else with respect—or not; that it's important to keep your word—or not. People who work with children *only* teach elementary school? Not in my book. As a parent, I found nothing unimportant about the work of adults who, by their every word and action, would ultimately teach my children that every child is a precious individual who ought to aim high—or that, as my son sadly learned, in school conformity is the greatest of all goods, that "You have to go along to get along," and that he will never be a "good" (i.e., conforming) student.

How is it that an elementary school teacher will gaze at the floor in response to the question "What do you do?" and denigrate his or her own work with that ugly word *only*? There are many answers to the question, among them several that lie in the realm of constructed consciousness, of a cultural value system teachers have inherited that has taught them that their work is far less important than that of doctors, of lawyers—and even, judging by income comparisons, less important than the work of plumbers.

Part of this devaluing certainly comes from the cultural legacies of teaching as women's work and of women's work as being less valuable than men's work. In a widely used foundations textbook, Joel Spring (1994) incorporates the following quotes to make that point. The first (from Elsbree, *The American Teacher*) comes from an 1841 document composed by the Boston Board of Education that argued for an increasing number of women in teaching:

As a class, they [women] never look forward, as young men almost invariably do, to a period of legal emancipation from parental control, when they are to break away from the domestic circle and go abroad into the world, to build up a fortune for themselves; and hence, the sphere of hope and of effort is narrower, and the whole forces of the mind are more readily concentrated upon present duties. (42)

Spring also includes an assertion made by Horace Mann, "the father of American education," in 1846: "Reason and experience have long since demonstrated that children under 10 or 12 years of age can be more genially taught and more successfully governed by a female than by a male teacher" (42).

Women, then, seem destined by nature and by natural restrictions to remain in roles defined and controlled by others, themselves controlling only still weaker groups like young children. After all, how much is there for young children to learn? Some letters and numbers, some simple information about days and months and years, about national holidays and heroes. How hard can that be? For a very long time, there has been a sort of generic mental confusion about the difference between teaching and babysitting. Although most people might deny it if asked outright, the truth is that culturally, teaching *is* most often confused with babysitting. When teachers strike, for example, parents often protest loudly about having to arrange child care while they work. At hostile meetings, parents demand an answer to the question "What am I supposed to do with these kids while you're home watching tv? I have to work, you know!"

Administrators sympathize. Good teachers feel guilty. But *why*? Why does the problem of what to do with children while teachers strike seem to belong to the teachers? Why is it teachers' responsibility to make sure that children are safe and cared for while parents work? When was parental responsibility for children's daytime welfare between the months of September and June transferred always and forever to teachers? And if it's difficult to make up school days missed because of strikes, is that because teachers refuse to teach after June 30, or because the state has passed a law defining the school year, or because parents don't want family vacation plans interrupted? Why are the schedules and convenience of everyone else more important than reasonable salaries and working conditions for teachers?

The idea that teaching amounts to child care pervades thinking about schooling and is reinforced when teachers refer to themselves as *only* teachers. It is an idea that is reinforced by the fact that so many people believe that teachers have their summers "off." It is reinforced by mothers who tell their daughters, "You know, teaching would be a great job for you. Kids always love you when you babysit, and your schedule will match your kids' when you have a family. You won't have to worry about what to do with them when they're not in school." It is reinforced by self-important school directors who pledge to their nieces and nephews who are earning straight Cs in college, "Don't worry. Just get your degree and I'll make sure you have a job." It is reinforced by arrogant college professors who tell their best students "you're much too smart to teach." It is reinforced by inept teacher educators who neither model nor insist on intellectualism and excellence in their classes.

Sadly, too many teachers do in fact play the role of well-paid babysitters who get the bonus of summers "off." They don't behave as professionals. They aren't knowledgeable, they don't model lifelong learning, they don't model dignity and respect for others, they waste instructional hours talking about their hobbies, they depend on worksheets and ten-year-old tests to do their "teaching" for them. They, too, contribute to the impression that teaching is babysitting, a job (rather than a profession) that takes little or no skill; that you don't need to be very bright to be a teacher; that teachers are often lazy and incompetent.

Truly good and professional teachers (the kind who spend nights and weekends and summers reading, thinking, rethinking. and planning) receive messages about how little their work is valued by the culture at large, especially by taxpayers who protest every salary increase vociferously, by parents who worry more about child care during strikes than the issues that caused them, by administrators who issue commands from on high without consultation, and by other teachers who ridicule dedication and who show movies every Friday because Thursday night is darts night at the town pub.

Men who teach elementary school suffer twice the stigma because not only is their work thought to be cheap and easy, but it's also thought to be beneath a man. Must be a pretty dumb or unambitious guy, the thinking goes, to want to be a *schoolmarm*. Or else, he must have some doubt about his sexual identity—better keep an eye on him. Despite the social revolution that has finally granted men the ability to change diapers, to cook a grilled cheese sandwich for the kids at lunch, and to read bedtime stories, relatively few men enter elementary education. Generally, in a class of thirty students, I might have three men. And I know my experience is not unusual. More men teach high school, but even there, the stigma lingers. In his classic text *High School*, Ernest Boyer reports a telling incident:

> One teacher, who works as a meat cutter during the summer, was told by a fellow butcher who discovered he was a teacher, "Man, that's a dead-end job. You must be a real dummy." (in Spring, 1996, 41)

As a result of teachers' constructed consciousness ("I am *only* a teacher"), administrators (who are nearly universally men) too often treat teachers as if they were themselves children, issuing orders to be executed without question: "You may or may not or will or will not do this and that and this in exactly this way and no other." Rather than launching an adult protest and challenging patronizing manifestos, teachers too often grumble to each other in the faculty lounge like children out of their parents' hearing—and then do as they're told.

Instead of insisting like adults that administrators do something about the incompetent down the hall showing movies every Friday, instead of pressuring unions so that they don't in fact function to protect incompetents, good teachers shrug off others' unprofessional behavior as being out of their control. They allow others to make decisions and policy without question and challenge. The result is often against their own best interests: administrators act like patronizing parents or omniscient dictators; incompetents perpetuate the image of teachers as lazy babysitters; and, the good teacher suffers public scorn along with the bad teacher, like a well-behaved child sent to detention with the whole class for some rowdiness he had no part in. "That's just the way it is," he shrugs on his way down the hall to be punished without just cause. "Life isn't fair."

That's just the way it is.

THAT'S NO LADY, THAT'S A STUDENT

Students, of course, fare even worse than teachers in school hierarchies. An absolute mania for control pervades school thinking and practice, making students little more than animals confined to a maze of restrictions. (Indeed, more often than any educator is likely to admit, "animals" is precisely the word teachers use to describe their students.)

From their earliest days in the classroom, students find blackboards filled with rules formulated by teachers before any class member set foot in the room. They learn they mustn't speak to each other or to the teacher unless the teacher lifts a ban on their talk. (Of course, teacher talk is the only important talk in the room, and so it fills most of the day.) Children are told where to sit, when to stand, what to do, and how to do it, except at recess. Even then, however, someone else decides if it's too cold or wet for them to be comfortable outdoors, whether they *will* go out or stay in (no individual preferences allowed), and what games may be appropriate in the schoolyard. The teacher decides when children should stop reading an interesting book or puzzling out a difficult math problem. The teacher decides which science lesson she thinks is interesting, and when it might be so for the children. The teacher or school decides when the children will eat or drink, sometimes selecting a time less than three hours after they've arrived and some four or five hours before they go home. In what seems to me the most bizarre rule of all, if among the most common, the teacher decides when it might be appropriate for a child to visit the bathroom and relieve him or herself. Even that most personal of all decisions is removed from the child's control.

In these ways, schooling teaches children that students are objects in schools, pegs moved about on someone else's gameboard. They learn not to expect to make decisions for themselves. They learn that their own opinions and views don't matter. They learn not to challenge authority or to experiment with new ways of doing things. "But I got the right answer!" wails the student who had a math problem marked wrong. "Yes, but you didn't do it the way I told you to," answers the all-powerful teacher. Conformity reigns, and creativity is often punished.

Unquestioning obedience and distrust of one's own feelings and intelligence is, of course, a mindset that many conservative parents would endorse. But most teachers don't perceive themselves as helping to build mental cages for their students. Quite the contrary: the rhetoric of schools and teachers most often talks about every student attaining his or her potential as a unique human being. In an odd sort of paradox, schools insist on uniformity and control as a means of creating conditions in which every student can learn, can achieve his or her own potential. And yet that insistence undermines their professed goals of empowering every student.

Every teacher who has worked with older children experienced in traditional schooling is familiar with the frustration of trying to get them to voice opinions and take stances. After children are silenced for years in elementary schools, junior and senior high school teachers often decide that students should suddenly have their own ideas and hold their own opinions. "Write about anything you want," the liberal English teacher says. "Like what?" students ask. "Design a unique project that shows how much you've learned," the teacher focused on outcomes urges. "I don't know what you want," the student whines. "What do you think of the federal government removing Native American children to boarding schools and forbidding them to use their native language?" I ask college freshmen, and they stare at me blankly, watching my face for a clue as to what I think they should think.

Children grow into the passive lumps high school teachers and college professors and employers complain about because school has taught the vast majority of young people that they are incompetent and that their thinking is neither interesting nor to be trusted. In a state of constructed consciousness, they come to believe that the terms "student" and "intelligent human being having human rights" are mutually exclusive descriptions. They allow teachers to bore them, to treat them with disrespect, to treat them unfairly without protest, because since they first set foot in school they have been taught that their voices are irrelevant.

I know a college student who wanted to change her major to get away from a professor who, in talking about the difficulty of telling what people are thinking from their facial expressions, said in class "Right now, for example, someone here might be thinking about sleeping with me." The fact that it seemed more reasonable to her to change her major than to complain about the professor's inappropriate example speaks volumes about students' perceptions of authority in the classroom.

I know another student, a single parent, who went to see a professor to explain why she couldn't go on a field trip he scheduled. "I can't afford to pay for that much child care," she said, "but I can get free care another day. I'll drive down to the museum on my own and I'll do any kind of report or activity you want to prove I did it." The professor's response? "I think you need to do some hard thinking and get your priorities in order." The student, believing the professor's take on the issue had to be the only legitimate one, left feeling guilty because she was an impoverished single mother and also feeling inadequate in the face of academic demands. He was a man; he had a degree and title; he sat in the front of the room. She must have been wrong to resist spending her meager grocery money on child care just so that she could do what he wanted at the exact moment he found most convenient.

Speculation on why schools are so insistent on top-down authority, control, and unquestioning obedience can, and has, filled volumes of other books. As Theodore Sizer speculates,

> Perhaps Americans don't want question-askers, people who want answers. Perhaps, in sum, the unchallenging mindlessness of so much of the status quo is truly acceptable: it doesn't make waves. (1984, 237)

Maybe accepting the status quo, not rocking the boat, letting well enough alone (for those who have enough to live comfortably on, anyway) is just what we expect our schools to endorse. Do we mean to train workers who will tolerate boredom, who will do as they're told, who will see themselves as disconnected from management decisions and corporate policies? Do we mean for most American citizens to think of themselves as not having voices that matter? Or, are school routines less sinister than that? Do we carry on past routines habitually and thoughtlessly, rather than manipulatively? If the results are the same, are we then blameless for bad outcomes simply because we can say "But I never *meant* for that to happen"?

Whatever the teacher believes is the rationale for schooling's mania for controlling students, it's difficult to dispute that much of what is done in classrooms teaches students to be seen and not heard. Teachers would do well to ask themselves whether this outcome matches their own intentions in working with students, and which of their practices effectively silence students. They would also do well to ponder why teachers themselves are often as powerless and voiceless in the face of administrators as students are powerless and voiceless in the face of teachers.

It is such hierarchies and privileged voices that the critical theorist calls our attention to and invites us to probe. Why is it, as the common saying has it, that schools are places where "Men rule women, and women rule children"? How did the power come to be distributed as it is? Why aren't there more challenges to the status quo? What is the nature of the constructed consciousness that enables such hegemony? Most of us look up the ladder of our environment and defer to those situated above us, despite a truth that Paulo Freire often notes: "Everybody knows something, and everybody doesn't know something." If that's true—and it is, since each of us knows best how the world looks through our eyes—then what is gained and what is lost when teachers and students are both silenced in the face of authority?

THE (CLOUDY) VIEW FROM THE TOP

In any discussion of hegemony and constructed consciousness, there is a danger of misrepresenting the state and intentions of the more powerful group. In the language of critical theory, the oppressors, or those groups holding power, can be as unaware of constructed consciousness and hegemony as the oppressed, those groups lacking power.

In any discussion of different limitations placed on men and women, for example, descriptions of the situation may make men seem like villains, consciously demeaning and mistreating women. But in fact, many men are not only unconscious of the elevated position they hold, but their intentions may be diametrically opposed to real world results. Men who mean to treat women as equals may dominate them despite their intentions, just as teachers who may intend to nurture students may silence them instead. The road to oppression, like the road to another hell, can be paved with good intentions.

It's relatively easy to see the truth of this in relationships between husbands and wives. Certain gender role expectations have been in place for so long that two partners may live them out automatically, without being consciously aware of unequal power relations. Communications researchers like Deborah Tannen have demonstrated that men and women nearly speak a different language. A man may say, for example, "I'll be home around six. Let's have steak for dinner." When his wife says, "OK," the husband assumes that she means what she says: that his suggestion is agreeable to her. Unless she tells him, which she is unlikely to do if she believes her job is to make her husband happy, he has no way of knowing that she already had chicken thawing, that the chicken won't keep until tomorrow, and that the decision to have steak means she has to cook two dinners instead of one so that the poultry won't spoil. In such cases, women "lose" in silent resentment and men "win" without even knowing that a battle of conflicting interests has occurred. After suffering a number of these voluntary losses, women often explode like shotguns, their violent anger triggered by some trivial event, their stunned husbands asking dumbly "But what did I do to deserve THIS?" Neither is fully aware of what's happened, and both suffer.

This is a mundane illustration, but the point is far from minor. In failing to recognize privilege or power that we may have inherited, we fail to see the consequences of our position and choices for others. We don't check to see the effects of our actions ("Let's have steak") because we're not aware that others perceive us as being more important or powerful ("I was planning on chicken, but if you want steak, we'll have steak").

People of color often, for example, try to call attention to privileges white Americans have that they don't. A six-foot-tall young white man can visit a black neighborhood without being stopped for questioning by the police. A white person in evening clothes can count on hailing a cab and having it stop. White women can walk into any beauty parlor and find appropriate hair care items and someone able to execute any hair style they might choose. Whites don't think of such freedoms as privileges because they've never gone without them. They are just more of the way things are. African Americans in parallel situations can count on none of the above.

Administrators and teachers are equally privileged, of course, though they may not recognize the ways in which they are. Most male administrators would be angry if anyone suggested that they were hired at least in part because they were men—but nothing but gender bias in the hiring process can explain the current levels of male principals and superintendents. More qualified women than ever have been credentialed in these fields, and yet the percentage of men in administrative positions remains well over ninety percent. (If you doubt this claim, do a quick mental count of male and female administrators in your regional districts.) And, by virtue of their job titles, teachers can demand respectful treatment from students, no matter how unprofessional and disrespectful they themselves may be in a classroom. Woe to the student who calls a teacher lazy, but teachers can call students lazy (and worse) with impunity. Woe, too, to the student who has a personal problem and comes in without homework, but the teacher can put off grading tests and papers for days or months with no penalty. As for "right" answers—only the teacher has a voice there, too.

Blind to the privilege of our positions, we exact certain forms of behavior from others, sometimes without recognizing the deference we've received, often without questioning by what right we get cooperation from others and what we owe in return. Since power operates in all things, we would do well to remember that a dictator who smiles and speaks courteously is no less a dictator; a "kind" slaveowner is no less a slaveowner. Having inherited all kinds of powers and privileges that have much more to do with the color of our skin or the title of our position than with our individual merit, the least we might owe is some consciousness of the power we have, how we got it, and how we use it. Critical theory asks us to examine our own place in the hierarchical scheme of things, trying to determine patterns of constructed consciousness and hegemony, as well as their cause and effect. Who defers to us? Whom do we defer to? Why? What are the consequences? How might things be otherwise?

THE ROOTS OF SCHOOLING'S CURRENT STRUCTURE

Many of the power relationships cemented in today's schools grow out of a philosophy that has permeated schooling for decades and that is rarely articulated. Today's adults (as well as today's students) have unconsciously absorbed this philosophy from their own experiences. Most teachers act on it without being aware that their actions reflect and sustain a particular philosophical view of the world. Still less are they aware of the many unintended consequences their classroom actions may have.

Because it's impossible to understand why schools are as they are without understanding the role of philosophy in shaping them, relevant philosophies are the subject of the next chapter.

Note

1. Earlier writing often referred to this concept as false consciousness.

Chapter Three

RETHINKING WHAT WE KNOW
Positivist and Constructivist Epistemology

Let us acknowledge that the objective or disinterested researcher is
always on the side that pays best.

Wendell Berry

QUESTIONING ASSUMPTIONS

Imagine a blustery speaker on school reform insisting that "our students
must know more when they leave school!" Now, imagine the audience's
likely response: nods of agreement? an enthusiastic "absolutely!" here and
there? Few listeners would hear anything to doubt or challenge in the
speaker's claim—except, of course, for the critical theorist, who frequently
examines the murky deep structure under the apparently simple surface
structure of everyday language. Working to uncover cultural assumptions,
the critical theorist asks of the speaker: "But what do you mean by *know*?
And what makes *more* necessarily better?"

However rarely such questions are asked, they are essential ones,
because embedded in common demands for students to "know more" are
philosophical definitions and assumptions that few educators have ever
consciously considered. Like many Americans who buy primarily
American music because that's what they hear on radio stations *they* listen
to (or like some other Americans who buy primarily Latin music because
that's what they hear on the radio stations they listen to), educators make
choices endorsing one particular perspective largely because they haven't
been exposed to an alternative. Though a world of music is available,
shoppers buy primarily the kind of music that surrounds them culturally;
they don't notice that their selections also involve a default decision not to
buy anything significantly different, like African or Asian music; they
don't notice that their choice implies that only the specific type of music
they buy is worthy of their interest and investment.

I've asked countless college students if they've ever listened to any African music, only to have them look at me as if I'd asked them whether they had ever dropped by Mars. Many opera devotees might react similarly to a question about rock. Of course, any individual human being might really enjoy one type of music and not the other as a matter of personal taste. But when whole hordes of people embrace the same wholesale exclusions—as in "What? Me listen to opera/rock? Are you crazy?"—then it seems likely that something cultural, rather than something personal, is shaping the choice.

Thus, being immersed in a culture, as earlier chapters detailed, limits our imagination and consequently affects our actions. When mainstream school culture limits how teachers conceptualize their work with students, teachers become limited in the classroom choices they make. In fact, teachers who believe they've created a classroom reflecting their individual goals may be no better off than people whose CD collection has been shaped entirely by what radio stations play. They consider only a limited menu, like CD buyers who choose between Smashing Pumpkins and Weezer, perhaps, or between Luciano Pavarotti and Placido Domingo—but never between Pumpkins and Pavarotti. They are unaware, too, that their "choices" implicitly endorse one specific perspective as being always and everywhere preferable to another—like rock fans and opera buffs who are equally scornful of the others' area, which they usually know nothing about.

As a specific radio station devotes itself to playing one type of music, schools devote themselves to breeding some particular kind of "knowledge." This must be so; if it weren't, school personnel couldn't ever talk about measuring what students know, a continuing preoccupation everywhere these days. If they want to measure "it," they must have *some* sense, conscious or not, of what "it" is.

Of course, any individual school's definition of "knowledge" and of what it means "to know" is usually implicit and unexamined. Like other cultural assumptions, the definition of "knowledge" is rarely explicitly discussed because it has been so long a part of the culture that it seems a self-evident truth to many, simply another part of the way things *are*. And, like other unconscious beliefs, this unexamined assumption limits our vision and has a profound impact on our actions.

The particular definition of knowledge a teacher assumes will shape her practice, consciously or not, because our definitions always shape our actions. If we define "good music" as rock, we buy one thing; if we define it as "opera," we buy another. Similarly, the mother who defines "a good breakfast" as "cereal the kids like" will buy Chocolate Captain Cavity with 53 g of sugar, whereas the mother who defines "a good breakfast" as "nutritious cereal, low in sugar" will buy whole grain Oaty O's with 2 g of sugar. Shoppers will buy one product or another based on how they define a "good" this or a "good" that—and teachers will teach one way or another, depending at least in part on how they define the "knowledge" they want their students to have, on what they mean when they say they want their students "to know" something.

But, no matter how routinely we take for granted the prevailing definition of "knowledge" embodied in common classroom practices, that definition is not a sacred truth. Instead, it reflects one very specific, dominant philosophical stance—to which there is an alternative. There are, in fact, two different epistemologies—that is, two different conceptions or definitions of knowledge—embodied in a variety of contemporary classroom methodologies. And therefore, to make genuine choices in their practice and to create a classroom that is philosophically coherent, educators need to understand both perspectives. They need to understand positivist epistemology, because it provides the foundation for traditional practice and is central to the "back to basics" movement. And, they need to understand constructivist epistemology as well, because it lies at the core of critical theory and is central to a variety of reform strategies currently being urged upon teachers.

WHAT EPISTEMOLOGY IS, AND WHY IT MATTERS

The formidable word "epistemology" sounds just like the kind of academic concern teachers frequently scorn: ivory tower stuff that has nothing to do with real world practice. Nothing could be further from the truth.

Epistemology is the branch of philosophy that seeks to define "knowledge," that seeks to explain what it means "to know" something, that seeks to understand how humans come to "know" things. Since all of schooling is about students coming to know things, what we mean by "knowing" is an essential question. Epistemology provides an answer to that question, and so it also provides an essential philosophical foundation for educational practice.

Choosing an epistemological position—that is, deciding which definition of "knowing" to accept—is much like choosing a destination, a goal to pursue. The New York driver who intends to travel to California must head her car west; she can gauge her progress along the way by checking the states she passes through against a map. But the New York driver heading for Florida, having an entirely different objective, must steer his car south and check his progress against a whole different set of states. While each might use exactly the same words to state their intentions ("to reach my destination"), their routes and checkpoints will be vastly different because their specific definition of "destination" differs.

It's useful, I think, to think of education in these terms of traveling toward a specific destination. While educators may use a common phrase to describe their goals—"to increase students' knowledge"—the specific way they define or conceptualize "knowledge" will involve goals as different educationally as California and Florida are geographically. And again educationally as well as geographically, vastly different goals dictate vastly different routes and assessment of progress.

My goal in this chapter is to give you sufficient understanding of different goals to choose consciously between them. Therefore, in the following sections, I'll first define positivist and constructivist epistemology and explain how the different definitions shape our vision of student learning. Then, I'll go on to discuss which methodologies and which assessments make sense for which stance. I invite you to keep your own thinking and practice in mind as you read, checking to see which camp your practice lies in now, whether you like it there, and whether your methods suit your intentions.

I hope you take this invitation for self-study seriously, because educators who have not identified their goals and checked their practice against them run the risk of trying to drive from New York to Florida via San Francisco. It simply makes no sense to use positivist methodology to reach constructivist goals, or vice versa. Unfortunately, few of us learn as undergraduates to choose our own philosophical destinations, to select appropriate pedagogical routes to them, and to monitor our activities for necessary course corrections. Teacher education programs have, alas, been much more likely to provide teachers-in-training predesigned Trip-Tiks than to teach them to be navigators in charge of their own classroom journeys. However, better late than never.

"JUST THE FACTS, MA'AM": POSITIVIST EPISTEMOLOGY

Simply put (too simply put, but we have to start somewhere), positivists conceptualize knowledge as a *thing*—essentially, as verifiable information born of scientific investigation. Certain facts, truths, relationships exist in the world; if we apply ourselves to exploring the world methodically, we can discover them. Knowledge is there, waiting for us to find it. The world is flat, or it is not; it is round, or it is not. When we can say with complete confidence that one or the other of these statements is true beyond any doubt at all, we have some "knowledge" about the earth's configuration. For a positivist, then, "knowledge" constitutes factual and verifiable information.

From this perspective, knowledge comes from science, whose job it is to discover truths about the world. To add to what we "know," researchers use a carefully monitored process they describe as "objective," seeking information that remains constant under stringent scientific scrutiny. Rigor in scientific methodology is intended to ensure that when science says something is so, we can count on the information, we can accept it as true. Specifically, scientists use an experimental method to determine the effect of variable a on subject b. When results are verified in trial after trial, the scientific community says it "knows" something new about the world. Employing this process, natural scientists (chemists, biologists, physicists) have compiled extensive information about the properties and the interaction of natural elements and forces.

Social scientists following the lead of natural scientists have also pursued the verifiable. They, too, have conducted experiments on the effect of variable a on subject b, extending the methodology of natural science to human sciences, including psychology and education. For example, educational researchers have pursued cause and effect questions like "What effect does time-on-task have on learning?" and "What effect does teacher wait-time have on student response?" (Educational research like this, conducted from a positivist perspective, is most commonly labeled *process-product* research. It is such research that has yielded prescriptions for specified amounts of time-on-task and wait-time.)

For positivists, the verifiable findings of scientific researchers comprise our "knowledge" of a subject—the trustworthy information about it we have to date, born of scientific investigation. If we keep in mind that positivists insist upon scientific verification of information, we can use the terms "knowledge" and "information" interchangeably in talking about the positivist perspective. We should note, too, that science also seeks to build theory upon the information it uncovers, but there is a clear distinction between "theory" and "knowledge." Something is not "known" until it has been demonstrated repeatedly under experimental conditions. Over the course of time, the sheer amount of information—of facts, of "knowledge"—that researchers have produced is virtually incomprehensible. An important educational question results from the production of so much information: Given all that we "know," how do we organize and share the knowledge that researchers have uncovered?

The apparently logical answer to this question has been to keep the verified facts that constitute what we know sorted into categories—chemistry, mathematics, grammar, music, history, and so on. While some of these fields are labeled "arts" or "humanities" rather than science, for the purposes of schooling they are treated the same: discrete areas where researchers pronounce what is known about the field. There is no distinction made in art history and chemistry textbooks to explain the different processes researchers used to determine the knowledge contained within their pages; each book presents the known facts of the field. Within universities, of course, the chemistry researcher may scorn the work of the art historian as not truly "research" (because it's not born of scientific method). Still, the general framework—"knowledge is information that is identified by experts who conduct research in the field"—is so firmly in place that the distinction between "science" and "not science" for the purposes of education never comes up in schools. That Beethoven was a great composer and Twain a great writer are presented as facts as credible as the fact that water freezes at 32° Fahrenheit.

Since each category (mathematics, science, English, music) is so large, each also contains multiple levels of subcategories to make information still more manageable—everything we know about verbs in one subcategory within the subcategory of grammar, for example, everything we know about Romantic composers in another subcategory within the subcategory of composers, and so on. Thus, all of the knowledge we have is neatly divided and subdivided to smooth the way for its acquisition by others, and the parameters that shape positivist "teaching" and "learning" and "schooling" are in place.

TRADITIONAL PRACTICE: POSITIVIST LEARNING

If knowledge consists of information, then "to know" means "to be familiar with what has been discovered/recorded by researchers/experts." "Knowing" means "having information about." If education is to ensure that students "know more" when they leave school than when they enter it, then the task of the school is to help the young acquire more and more of the information that experts have already discovered and categorized. The task of teachers is to become somewhat expert in what is known, and then to pass information along to their students. The higher the grade level taught, the more expert the teacher must be in subject matter (ultimately culminating, of course, in the university professor/researcher who is expert in all that is known in her field and responsible for helping to conduct research in order to uncover new knowledge).

Traditional school practices reflect this conception of knowledge, teaching, and learning. Curriculum, for example, is organized around discrete subjects (math, English, history, music, art) and each subject functions as a sort of bin of important facts in the field. Exactly which facts are worth knowing and exactly how they should be arranged sequentially are decisions usually made by experts outside K-12 schools, because they are more familiar with the range of subject matter. Students have math lessons to learn about math, history lessons to learn about history, and lessons in different subjects are usually as isolated from each other as are the experiments of chemists and psychologists.

In addition, the whole of what students are to learn in the course of their schooling is divided into year-by-year plans: these things in first grade, followed by these in second, and so on. (In college, the division is into discrete courses, numbered at different levels: the 100 courses, followed by the 200 courses, and so on.) The assumption is that subcategories can be used to organize lessons and that the student's "knowledge" about a subject will be cumulative: first letters, then words, then sentences, then paragraphs, and then essays, with each bit cemented on top of the bit that came before, like bricks in a wall. Textbooks support this structure by keeping different bits of information neatly sorted into and confined within different grade level and/or subject matter texts.

It is very early in school years when subject matter is considered significantly specialized and difficult to require teachers with some expertise in a specific subject matter. In many schools, elementary students in very low grades are with one teacher for math and science, another for language arts and social studies, another for art, and another for music. Walls between subject matter are usually as firm as those enclosing the schoolhouse: the reading teacher tells children not to ask him math questions, and the math teacher informs the principal that she cannot be expected to teach writing.

The positivist conception of knowledge as some independent and objective *thing* also permeates common language about teaching and learning. We talk about a "body of knowledge" as if it were a physical smorgasbord for students to ingest. We talk about "acquiring" or "getting an education" as if it were analogous to strolling through the produce section and picking up a package of celery. We talk about next year's lessons "building on" this year's, as if teachers were all subcontractors: the plumber waiting for the mason to finish the foundation before putting in the pipes, the carpenter waiting for the plumber to finish putting in the pipes before putting up the drywall. Teachers talk about "covering" material as if they were walking from one corner of a rug to another. All such images invoke the perception of knowledge as a *thing*. If it is a thing, then we can also talk about some people having it and others not having it (just as some people have heaps of money and others don't); we can talk about who knows more than someone else. We can also say that the goal of education is for those who do have it (teachers) to pass their knowledge on to those who don't (students).

Brazilian educator and theorist Paulo Freire has a memorable metaphor for this conception of knowing and teaching and learning, which he refers to as "banking" pedagogy (1970, 58). Teachers, or experts, first acquire heaps of information, the currency of the classroom. When teaching classes, they deposit the information that they have, the facts that they know, into students. Testing constitutes withdrawal, a process of extracting from students the same information deposited in them during classes. The teacher, then, functions as banker, making deposits and withdrawals, and he also provides grades as a kind of bank statement indicating how much "knowledge" was successfully transferred from him into each student's account. It is a very different conception than that held by constructivists.

MAKING SENSE OF FACTS: CONSTRUCTIVIST EPISTEMOLOGY

I've attempted to define constructivist epistemology more times than I can count to more people than I can count. This involves explaining that "knowledge" can be defined as something very different from verifiable facts—the definition unconsciously held by nearly every educator exposed to and using traditional practices. Because the constructivist perspective is so alien for so many, I've had a lot of practice finding a beginning point that a majority of nonphilosophers finds accessible. Experience has taught me that one dependable gateway into this unfamiliar mental territory is a personal anecdote that strikes a familiar chord for many people. Ergo and forthwith, oversimplifying yet again: here is the story of an old skirmish between my husband, Ed, and my Aunt Wanda.

On our way home from an afternoon visit, Ed and I compared impressions that Aunt Wanda had cold-shouldered him during our conversation. She largely ignored his remarks and had a distinct edge in her voice when she had to address him for some reason. "What did I do?" he asked. "Beats me," I answered. "I'll go down for lunch tomorrow and try to find out for you."

Lunch was revealing, and my subsequent after-dinner talk with Ed touchy. The facts were clear: Ed had not invited Aunt Wanda and Uncle Frank to see our regional Triple A baseball team play once all summer, despite the fact that his company has season tickets and despite the fact that he knows they both love baseball. The season was over, and we had not taken them to a single game. What was not so clear was what exactly these facts meant. To my relatives, the facts added up to only one thing: Ed was an insensitive and ungrateful twerp. The things Aunt Wanda and Uncle Frank have done for us and our children over the years are countless, involving vastly generous amounts of time, energy, and sometimes money. They rarely leave their farm. She doesn't drive, and they both prefer he not drive if it can be avoided. They are both delighted and quick to accept when someone invites them out, especially for something like an afternoon or evening of baseball. Given that context, only an insensitive and ungrateful twerp would have failed to invite them to a game.

Ed didn't see it precisely this way. In the summer, he works six or seven days a week, twelve or more hours a day. An avid golfer, he'd found precious few hours for golf over the entire summer. He was often so tired that he was in bed half an hour after he ate dinner. Baseball was the *last* thing on his mind. If they *wanted* to see a game, why didn't they just *ask* us? (I knew what my aunt would say: "He *knows* we love baseball—why should we have to ask?") From Ed's perspective, he was innocent of the charge of thoughtlessness, and they were guilty of being unreasonable and insensitive.

The facts were indisputable; it was the meaning of them that was open to interpretation ("You're a thoughtless twerp." "No, you're insensitive and unreasonable."). Which picture seemed more true depended upon whether you were the person sitting around the back porch bored all summer instead of munching peanuts at a ball game, or you were the guy answering telephones and solving logistical problems for a fleet of trucks and men scattered all over the East Coast 70 or so hours a week.

The point of this anecdote is no great revelation: of course the way humans perceive things is influenced by their personal circumstances and personal views of the world. That's why we generally make a distinction between "opinion" and "fact." People look at facts—at what others do or don't do, at what they say or don't say, and how—and then they decide for themselves what those facts mean.

For the constructivist, it is the *meaning assigned to facts*, rather than the facts themselves, that matters when we talk about *knowledge*, about *knowing* something. When we have only the facts of my family dispute, how much can we say we "know" about it? The facts are inert and meaningless until we attempt to interpret them, until we try to add them up into some coherent picture. No, my aunt and uncle weren't invited and didn't go to a baseball game. The important question here is "So? What does *that* mean?" To genuinely "know" what's going on, we have to understand the situations of both parties, how their past experiences shaped their expectations and actions, and so on.

For the constructivist, not just personal dispute but all knowledge is a matter of human interpretation. "Knowledge" is not something existing independently in the world just waiting for us to find it; instead, "knowledge" comes into being only when a human being examines data (facts, artifacts, and so on) and assigns meaning to it. Knowledge consists not of the facts themselves (which critical theorists often pointedly refer to as "factoids"— untrustworthy, decontextualized bits of information). Instead, knowledge is the sense that humans make of factual information. In the words of John Mayher, "*there is no knowledge without a knower*" (79).

Consider, for example, the difference between a student being able to *say* or *write* "two plus two equals four" and genuinely understanding what the words "two" and "plus" *mean*. As any teacher who has ever taught a vocabulary list of any kind knows, the fact that a student can repeat a definition does *not* necessarily mean the student has any understanding of what the word signifies, of what the word *means*. What good are the words (the names, the dates, the formulas) if they don't accompany personal understanding?

Consider the fact that Spanish missionaries traveled to California and worked to introduce Native Americans to Christianity and farming. So? What does that fact tell us? Does it mean that the missionaries were earnest moral men who dedicated their lives to saving the souls and improving the lives of the Native Americans? Or, that they were arrogant cultural imperialists who destroyed cultures while mouthing pieties and concurrently developing the near equivalent of slave labor? Without context and interpretation, the bare fact is meaningless, inert.

It is also a fact that grammatical rules of standard English call for regular third person singular verbs to have an s at their end. So? Does that mean that everyone in the United States is somehow morally obligated to say *she walks* or *he talks* rather than *she walk* or *he talk* every time they speak—even in informal situations? Or, does it mean that a person whose speech and writing conform to that rule in formal, public situations will be thought smarter than someone who doesn't? Again, of what use are facts if they aren't presented to us in some context, if they don't *mean* something to us? What good is a rule if we don't know where it came from, when and where and why we might choose to follow it? Only when we can make sense of facts and rules, only when we have some personal understanding of data, can we say we *know* something.

The constructivist, then, insists that "knowledge" is *constructed* by human beings when they assign meaning to data; it is not simply sitting out in the world waiting for us to find it. No one "knows" anything until he can add separate bits of data up into a coherent, meaningful picture for himself. Predictably, then, in constructivist education, information takes a back seat to student *processing* of information.

LESS IS MORE: CONSTRUCTIVIST LEARNING

Since the constructivist doesn't perceive knowledge to be an external thing, the constructivist teacher doesn't believe knowledge is something she possesses, something that she can simply hand off to (or deposit in, or transmit to) students. Instead, the task of the constructivist teacher is to design experiences that will give students an opportunity to develop their own understanding of the data at hand. The teacher's goal is for students to use information in some way that will deepen their own understanding of an area. Whether or not all students have precisely the same experience is often irrelevant; what matters is that every student's personal understanding is moved forward.

While there may be reasons for a group of students to read the same novel, for example, there is no need for all of them to read the same novel in order to learn about theme, or about characterization, or about dialogue, or about any other element of literature. Students can apply the same question to a variety of novels, share their answers with each other, and learn a great deal. The teacher might say something like "This time, let's give some thought as to how an author might choose to begin a novel, why one author might start with scenery and another with a dramatic event." In this case, if every student were reading a different novel and each read the first paragraph of his or her novel aloud, there would be a great deal of data for students to analyze. It doesn't matter *which* novel a student reads; what matters is that the student comes to understand that authors make choices among certain devices in order to try and affect the reader this way or that. The focus in this example is on the student's increasing sophistication as a reader, not on the content of a specific work.

Since I'm a constructivist teacher, my foundations course offers multiple examples of my concern with process and understanding rather than with regurgitation of fact. The foundations textbook I use, for example, explains different types of power arrangements between school boards and communities, between school boards and superintendents, and among school board members themselves. I might require my students to memorize the information—a typical positivist task, since the positivist equates having information with knowing. Instead, I require my students to attend a school board meeting and to characterize it according to the information in their texts. Which type of power structures do they think they saw? What specific events or factors support their interpretation? How do they think this arrangement functions to promote or impede the good of the community? In effect, my students must apply their own intelligence and the information they have at hand to construct their own understanding of an event they witnessed themselves. Students freely choose the meetings they will attend, meaning that they will work with different data and construct different understandings of events. But being a constructivist, I am not concerned with the exact data a student works with and the exact answer a student formulates. My question is "can the student apply her intelligence and this information to data and formulate a sensible interpretation of the whole event?" If so, then I would say that the student has learned something about power and school boards, that the student now "knows" something she didn't before. I don't especially care if students memorize the formal terms in their texts, because they can always look that information up if they need it.

Again, constructivist teachers are concerned with process, not product. They are concerned with individual renderings of personal understanding, knowledge they have constructed for themselves, not lockstep regurgitation of reified fact. They don't care which formula a student uses to solve a problem as long as the student can explain why a given formula works, or why two different formulas work. The focus is not on facts nor on "right" answers, but on how students process facts, on what meanings students can construct using the facts at hand, on how they make sense of information they receive.

The positivist teacher says a student "knows" a Frost poem when the student knows what expert critics say it means; the constructivist teacher says a student "knows" a Frost poem when he can make sense of it for himself, when he can articulate an interpretation that fits with the actual words of the poem—whether any critic has ever endorsed that interpretation or not. Whether a student can *do* something sensible with information, rather than whether a student can repeat information on demand, is the constructivist teacher's concern.

POSITIVIST METHODOLOGY AND ASSESSMENT

When a positivist teacher says she wants her students to "know more," she is essentially talking about having more information, about giving the students more of what she, the expert, knows. Therefore, a logical characteristic of positivist education is the teacher lecture (teacher talk). Books provide some information, and the expert teacher clarifies or extends this information for students. Students talk little because they are the ones who don't know the subject yet; what can they contribute to classroom talk? When they do talk, then, it is usually so that the teacher can check to see whether information is being retained: "So, then, John, what were the three causes of that battle?" "So, then, Mary, what does X stand for in this case?" Students listen, and they take notes—often in exactly the same words as the teacher or the text used. They do the same tasks over and over ("Write these spelling words ten times. Underline the nouns in these sentences.") so that they remember what the teacher or text has told them.

Work comes from a predetermined curriculum, selected by experts who know even more than the teachers: this list of spelling words this week, that list next week. These historical facts this month, those historical facts next month. Based on the grade level textbook, we get teacher talk and teacher plans: "Do this factual, multiple choice (fill-in-the-blank or short answer) worksheet. Do the questions at the end of the chapter. Tell me what the book says. Tell me what I said yesterday. Memorize this. That will be on the test. You have to know it because I said so, or you have to know it because you'll need it next year (or in high school, or when you get to college—can't put the walls up before the foundation is poured!)."

Even "personal opinion" questions have "right" answers. Once, for example, after reading a far-fetched story about a little boy home alone who experienced every conceivable household fiasco possible, from a foaming and flooding dishwasher to a wet St. Bernard escaping from the bathtub, my son had to answer questions at the story's end. One asked, "Have you ever had a day like this?" My son's answer was "No, I have never had a day like this." The teacher gave him no credit for that response. *BZZZZZTT!!*: *"Sorry, boy—wrong opinion!"*

Assessment is based on tests, and the test questions have one right answer (a fact is a fact—1492 is not 1493). The teacher is the sole authority, the only expert on knowledge: "I don't care if your answer made sense to you, I say *this* is the right answer and *I'm* the teacher, and so you're wrong and

I'm right." Scores are in numbers, and a 68 is not a 70, and the student who earned an 85 surely "knows more" than the 68 and 70 students.

Learning—that is, memorizing—is hard work, drudgery of sorts. Generally, positivist teachers would agree that "We can't expect students to enjoy it. They'll need carrots and sticks, and at least once in a while we'll probably have to break down and play Jeopardy or something so that they can feel like there's *some* fun in school, anyway." In a positivist classroom, good students are students who listen carefully, who repeat what they've read and heard faithfully. They don't challenge the teacher's authority, and they don't question that what the teacher says is true or important. A positivist classroom is predictable, orderly, sequential, and managed by the teacher, who is the most important and knowledgeable person in the room.

CONSTRUCTIVIST METHODOLOGY AND ASSESSMENT

The constructivist classroom offers a stark contrast to the positivist one. When a constructivist teacher says she wants her students to "know more," she is essentially talking about increasing students' ability to make sense of information; she doesn't imagine transferring information to students because she believes all learners must work to develop individual understanding of facts at hand.

Because students need to build their own understanding of information and ideas, their interests and experience are very important to classroom life. In the example above about reading novels, students are allowed choice so that the novel they read is interesting to them. If it is interesting to them, then it will be easier for them to use their own responses to see how authors try to orchestrate readers' responses to the book. If the task is to learn about how novels are constructed, any well-constructed novel is suitable. Later, even ill-constructed novels can help students learn about judging the merit of different books—what's trite, what's innovative; what's predictable, what's pleasantly surprising to the experienced reader.

No doubt some of you are already worried about core experiences and will be protesting here that there must be some books all students must read, that there must be some events all students must know about. Please note that I have not said that students should never consider the same information, simply that it is not essential for them to always use the same data to develop an understanding of a single concept. There is no reason that one student can't explore division by counting out cookies while another counts out candy corn, and there is no reason that one student can't explore foreshadowing in a Poe novel while another explores it in a Stephen King novel. Every student might read Poe—or they might not. It depends on what sort of understanding the teacher hopes to encourage.

Following individual interest remains important even when a single area of information is considered essential to students. If students are not somehow personally engaged in a task that holds some relevance or interest for them, they are not likely to be able to construct a personal understanding of information. As a university writing teacher, for example, I was responsible for being sure that all of my students knew how to complete and incorporate library research into a paper. I never saw any reason (except, possibly, for my own convenience) for every student to do library research at exactly the same time. Now, I think it's useful to learn about library research—but certainly not for its own sake. A writer goes to the library when she feels strongly about a topic, wants to write persuasively about it, and absolutely must be thoroughly knowledgeable with the pros and cons of the topic at hand. Therefore, I gave students some information on when they might choose to do library research and then left them to decide *when* in the semester the paper they were working on required some outside expertise. They had to do it sometime, but when and why were up to them.

This was because I would not have said my students knew about library research if they merely had information about how to do it. What good would it have done for them to be able to look up journal articles if they never understood when a writer might incorporate research into a piece, if they couldn't identify times in their own writing experience when a trip to the library would be useful? And how could they have understood a need for research if I didn't allow them to discover one in their own unique experience? For a student to remember that I said research is useful is not the same as that student coming to understand for himself, through personal experience, when and where and why research is useful.   And understanding cannot be assigned or memorized.

In the constructivist classroom, talk—spoken or written—is an essential part of learning. Teachers who have ever said "You know, I confess that I never really understood this subject/topic until I started teaching it" can refer to their own experience for evidence that putting ideas into words is crucial to learning. It is when we try to find words for our understanding that we are forced to grapple with pinning our sometimes vague ideas down into specific, coherent statements of meaning. This is exactly why most of us find writing so difficult. Often, it is only after the ordeal of trying to clearly say or write what we know that we come to really understand it. And often, in trying to say what we know, we discover just how much we don't yet know or understand.

For this reason, students in constructivist classes spend most of their time writing, talking with others, or working on projects that involve personal interaction. Teachers and texts do, of course, offer information. However, every student talks far, far more than he listens to the teacher, who spends most of his time working with individuals or small groups. Small group tasks, "pair and share," journal writing, learning logs, and discussion groups are all common ways for students to talk about the ideas in their heads. Students or groups may work to explain information from the text in their own words, or to formulate questions about the implications or applications of specific information, or to tackle any one of countless tasks that engage students in working with the information they've received, with processing that information in some way that reveals its point, its relevance, its usefulness.

In most cases, individual student writing and talk, rather than tests, signal to the teacher whether learning has occurred. An elementary school teacher might, for example, ask students in class one day to explain in writing what it means to "add" something, to "divide" something, what a decimal point is, or why a sentence includes a verb. The student who can explain in her own words what "add" means and who can invent and complete three or four addition problems demonstrates a thorough understanding of the concept of "addition." What would a test with 30 problems prove that such writing doesn't?

Consider the following student math definitions, taken from a teacher-written text on how to use writing to promote learning.

A decimal point divides a whole number from parts of one number—Chris.

A decimal is like a period but it separates numbers from each other— Earl.

It [a decimal] separates the holes from part of a hole— James.

Why? You round because you have to. Rounding is part of math that you have to know. You round when the book says to round. Rounding you have to know! Rounding isn't hard. Some of the numbers you round is in trillions. How? You can round every number in math. The control number is the number on weather you can stay or go up one— Patty. (Owen 1987, 25)

Is there any question which students have conceptual understanding of decimal points and which don't? Or that Patty does not yet understand rounding? Is there any question which students might be allowed to work on an independent project and which students might be called to an in-class conference with the teacher, or with a student whose understanding is firm?

Generally and logically, then, constructivist teachers orchestrate different experiences for different students at different times, and they support portfolio assessment rather than standardized, objective tests. Writing like that described and demonstrated above, often completed on something as informal as an index card, immediately tells the teacher who has "gotten" it and who hasn't, who needs to be engaged in more work with addition or decimals tomorrow, who can work concurrently on other projects. The individual writing, rather than a whole class test, goes into a portfolio, along with a variety of other tasks, to demonstrate progress toward individual understanding.

If the constructivist teacher should give a test, it's usually an essay exam, centered on a question that asks students to add discrete bits of information up into a coherent big picture. In my foundations course, for example, I might ask:

Using the traits described in your text as a starting point, explain which characteristics of a *professional* you believe you already exhibit and which you will need to cultivate before you enter teaching. Include anecdotes from your own experience to support your analysis.

Much more often than such essay tests, however, student-designed projects are assigned to ensure that students have learned enough about a topic to *use* the information in some way. For example, when I taught business writing, I asked students to identify a piece of writing they had needed since coming to the university, but which they found incomprehensible (perhaps an explanation of the university's policy on a diversity course requirement) and to work with the appropriate campus office to make a more useful document available to students.

Or, in some cases, students chose to compose new documents, as in the case of the student who researched long-distance telephone rates. She eventually wrote a brochure explaining which company offered the best rates for certain kinds of calling habits; the brochure was subsequently distributed by the student affairs office and widely used by resident students choosing a long distance service. The point in every project was to be able to discriminate between clear and confusing writing, to identify a particular need for a clear (or more clear) document, and then to use the skills developed in class to produce a useful document. Everyone wrote something different, but every project demonstrated the same kinds of understanding and skill.

In schools that have endorsed constructivist philosophy, curriculum is often interdisciplinary and theme-based. Constructivists perceive walls between subjects as a sometimes convenient fiction. The walls are fictional because everywhere, subjects overlap: can literature and history really be neatly separated, for example? But walls are sometimes convenient as an aid in focusing our attention as we work on logistics. For example, having a category of literature described as "The Lost Generation" makes it easier for us to answer the question "Which novel might students read to get a sense of the country's mood after World War I?" Still, the overriding goal in every classroom is to enable students to tie disparate information into some coherent, personally meaningful whole, and so visible subject walls are beginning to crumble in constructivist classrooms.

For example, I was once a frequent visitor to a New York City school during a marking period when every class was exploring the theme of *power*. Humanities classes (where students spent one third of their day) read, talked, and wrote about such phenomena as war and political elections. Concurrently, quantification classes (where students spent another third of their day) explored such topics as how science has given us power over our natural environment (as well as over countries with less sophisticated weapons), and how various kinds of statistics and mathematical graphics can be manipulative and confer ill-deserved authority. (The third part of the day was spent in a variety of activities, including such options as internships and community service.)

A WORD ON CRITICISMS

As I wrote this chapter, I received electronic mail from a colleague who advises a student group that was sponsoring a speech on "objectivism." There are many "good faith" educators who worry terribly about the constructivist's lack of faith in the "objectivity" that they believe science represents. They fear that constructivists have elevated what this colleague termed "whim" to the status of "knowledge," and that constructivists are undermining a solid, stable, dependable world with an irrational world view (or paradigm, another word common in the language of educational philosophy).

Their concerns will, no doubt, echo many objections that educators steeped in positivist tradition are likely to have had as they read through the above sections. "But 1492 is *not* 1493," they may have challenged above, "and science *is* objective and dependable." And, therefore, an additional word on why constructivists have rejected positivism seems in order here.

Facts, notes the constructivist, do not ever exist in a vacuum. Certain facts are uncovered because some scientist decided to research a specific area, and certain facts find their way into textbooks because some expert found those particular facts important. But scientists and experts are, when all is said and done, human—and no human can make a decision about what's important without using a particular world view to sift through what's available. It's impossible to do such sorting "objectively," because every human is immersed in at least one culture, and our culture shapes our perceptions. Any fact presented to us, then, necessarily comes to us filtered through someone else's vision.

The positivist would acknowledge that perspective shapes perception, and then would point out that that's precisely the difference between what we *know* from science and what we simply *think about* things. It's because human perception is so untrustworthy that scientific method is so important: in order to get information we can count on, the process of identifying it must be completely objective. We can't have any human opinions mucking up the process, clouding the knowledge that's out there in the world with a personal perspective. Positivists believe that scientific method is a corrective for unreliable humanity. If human bias were allowed into the process, the results would no longer be trustworthy. The objective researcher doesn't dabble in such matters as the ethics of California missionaries; he is interested only in the facts of the historical event. Science is in the business of *knowing*, not evaluating. If we're talking about judgments, then we're out of the arena of science and verifiable knowledge.

For example, the positivist is fully aware that an industrial farmer is going to *think* differently than an environmentalist, and that these two are likely to disagree on how much weed killer is too much to spray on crops. It's the job of scientists to focus on the verifiable "this much of this substance will or will not kill these weeds; this much of this substance will or will not affect human breathing." Science is one thing, policy quite another. But here the constructivist asks: "And just how do we keep the human perspective out of science when every scientist is human?" Consider this farming example. The work of the scientist researching weed killers is shaped by a cultural assumption that it's best for a society to have huge, commercial farms largely managed by technology rather than for communities to grow native crops and be more self sufficient. If we weren't in the cultural habit of shipping strawberries from California to Pennsylvania, there might have been less research done on preservatives and on chemical coolants for refrigerated trucks.

And, if *someone* weren't paying for research in these areas, they might have gone unexplored. How are we to think of science as objective, asks the constructivist, when areas worthy of research are determined by money provided by government, industry, and other special interest groups? To what extent has government-funded research, or lack of research, on cancer and on the AIDS virus been determined by political climate? Do we imagine that the tobacco industry is going to use its enormous resources to support research on drugs to help smokers kick a nicotine habit? Is a Catholic government likely to support research on birth control pills, or a Jewish government likely to support research on pork tenderizers? Scientists cannot research projects no one will fund. They find what they find because someone, somewhere, for some reason of her own is interested in having certain kinds of information uncovered. There is nothing at all objective about the funding process that shapes research agendas

And, the individual humanity of the scientist further biases the process. Much of science involves visual observation—and what we report seeing is conditioned by what we expect to see. Didn't man once know for a certainty that the sun revolved around the earth? The data didn't change; scientists found otherwise only when they were able to imagine that things *could* be otherwise, a cultural heresy at the time. Other such revolutions have occurred in physics and other areas. Listening to National Public Radio recently, in fact, I heard a report that some scientists claim to have discovered a "new" bone in the head; asked how it was possible the bone might have gone unnoticed for so long, the researchers responded that no one saw it because no one expected to see it there. Also, they explained, for as long as anyone in the field can remember, there has been only one way to dissect a skull. With open minds (or minds desperate to find something new, I don't know) this pair attempted a new method of dissection. As a result, they report that they have perceived something that no one claims to have perceived before.

Our attention is selective and our language imprecise, or precise in ways that affect our perception. For example, in a northern culture where snow is a critical element of everyday life, the person having six words available to describe different kinds of snow literally *sees* the falling snow differently than someone who knows only one word to describe it. Fine points in the language prompt this observer to attend to different characteristics of snow than does the English speaker who has only one word to name it. But even in English, a skier watching for a chance to hit the slopes will attend to—will actually look at and see—the texture of falling snow differently than a nonskier, or than a sixteen-year-old driver with no winter driving experience.

Being human, scientists cannot escape language and perceptual influences, no matter how stridently they may insist on their objectivity. The constructivist says to the scientist: "You do not live in a vacuum." Science is no less steeped in its own assumptions than any other culture; it is no less vulnerable to the influences of historical assumptions and values, as well as constraints of human perception and specific language systems. There are verifiable facts in the world, all right, but to insist that science is thoroughly objective, untainted by culture and the humanity of its workers, is to engage in wishful thinking.

CONSTRUCTIVISM AND CRITICAL THEORY

All constructivists are not critical theorists. However, *all critical theorists are constructivists.* The difference lies in how various groups define the purpose of education. A liberal constructivist, for example, might say that students must become skilled readers so that they can read newspapers and magazines thoughtfully, offer articulate opinions to representatives in government, and vote wisely in elections. A person can call himself a constructivist and also endorse many cultural maxims. For example, the educator who is a liberal constructivist might want a student to be able to detect bias in such magazines as *Newsweek* and *Time,* without thinking more deeply about the nature and effect of the bias.

The characteristic that sets critical theorists apart from other constructivists is an insistence that there is no part of the status quo that should not be challenged. The critical theorist will encourage students not only to recognize how a magazine report might be slanted, but will also ask "What accounts for this particular bias in this particular story, or magazine? Who gains what, who loses what, when the facts are added up this way? Whose version of this story hasn't been told? Why are these two particular magazines so widely read, and how significant are their differences? What can we learn if we look into which stories these magazines are *not* reporting?"

In short, critical theorists are very different from other constructivists in their constant search to discover whose choices account for the status quo and how things might be otherwise. They are interested not only in different interpretations that might be made of data, but in the way one account of facts or events—one narrative—privileges some people over other people, how it benefits some to the detriment of others. The critical theorist is aware not only that Native Americans can be named either "savages" or "victims," but also that to name them one way benefits the Caucasians who now own what was formerly tribal land, and to name them the other way suggests that an injustice might have been done and reparation owed. Every story is *someone's* story, every truth is *someone's* truth, and it is dangerous to accept any version of anything without asking "Whose story is this? Why are they seeing the data this way? What other meaning might these facts suggest?"

When thinking about this aspect of critical theory, I often remember the fable of the three blind men and the elephant. Because one could feel only the trunk of the elephant, one only a leg, and one only the tail, each had a very different idea of what an "elephant" was. Like a snake, said one; like a tree, said another; like a rope, said the third. Each was "right," and each was also "wrong." Their perceptions had to be combined and reconciled to formulate anything approaching a reasonable representation.

Critical theorists believe we are all in the position of blind men, limited in our individual perspectives. Before we can begin to claim to "know" anything, we have to consider what a variety of others can tell us. No one else can give us a single accurate picture of what the world "is," what is "important" in it: we have to construct our own understanding of the world for ourselves, basing it on a variety of sources. The facts of science are only one set of facts, American history only one of many global histories. We need to be informed by science, but also by art. We need to hear the voices of men, but also of women who have been traditionally silenced. We need to listen to those who speak standard English impeccably, but also to those who do not. Each of them has a perspective we can't see for ourselves, and only by adding their vision into our own can we begin to understand the multiple realities that actually exist in the world. To pretend to students that a single world view can be "accurate" and to ignore the ways different views privilege different people is to distort their vision in the guise of "educating" them.

The critical theorist's stance and goals are, of course, fully antithetical to traditional positivist education with its monolithic curriculum and its "right answer" orientation. A critical education based on constant questioning is diametrically opposed to lockstep ingestion of fossilized facts. It seeks above all to give students practice in examining existing power arrangements. Some Americans can order $93,000 dinosaurs from a Neiman Marcus catalogue while others beg coins for food. Some people are told what to do, and others tell them what to do. Some make decisions, others live with the results.

The culture is full of explanations. People who work hard get rich, lazy people don't. Smart people get good jobs, dumb people don't. If you want to keep your job, you have to learn to do as you're told. And on and on and on. Always, the critical educator asks "Do you believe that? Why? How did you come to believe it? Who does it benefit for you to believe that? What is the cost to you if you believe that? How else might you explain what's happening? Who would gain, who would lose, if this alternative view were accepted?"

Whereas the positivist believes that a single verifiable reality exists, *believes* that we can pile up and pass on to students a body of knowledge, the critical theorist denies that very possibility. Because of this difference in perspective, the critical educator prompts students constantly to question the status quo, the "official" or "accepted" account of events on which positivist practice is based. Therefore, critical theory and traditional, positivist practice are in opposition on every count—predictably and especially in the areas of classroom approach and authority, the subjects of the next two chapters.

Chapter Four

RETHINKING ED PSYCH 101
Instrumental Rationality and Post-Formalism

The structural arguments of Tyler, Schwab, and Bloom et al. . . . take ideological positions while denying ideology [and] offer advice about correcting practice that reinforces practice in place. . . . Why are they privileged? If these arguments fail to do what they claim, what ends do they serve? They serve to reproduce educational practices in the name of change and progress.

Cleo H. Cherryholmes

QUESTIONING UNQUESTIONED PREMISES

The pervasive, positivist orientation to education discussed in the last chapter has generated a massive educational infrastructure that is rarely acknowledged or questioned. Positivist assumptions underpin countless educational activities routinely accepted as part of "the way things are." If pressed for a more detailed rationale explaining why lesson plans list behavioral objectives, or why vocabulary words are routinely introduced before reading selections in textbooks, or why standardized tests are considered so reliable, an educator might well produce an explanation taken from educational psychology: "Well, Tyler's research on planning indicated . . . " or "According to Bloom's Taxonomy, . . . " or "In an ed psych course, I learned that . . ."

But in response to such answers, the ever-skeptical critical theorist asks "So what assumptions did *their* work embody? Why are *their* answers accepted as authoritative? What are the alternatives?" An exploration of those critical questions indicates that the most commonly cited authorities of educational psychology based their research and theories on premises that are positivist at their core—including even Piaget, who believed that humans construct their own understandings of the world. To enable substantive educational reform, not just some cosmetic surgery, it's necessary to understand how these unchallenged positivist assumptions have influenced educational psychology and subsequently shaped what is now routine practice in classrooms and districts nationwide.

PHILOSOPHICAL DIFFERENCES IN THE KITCHEN

When my son received the results from a standardized reading test he had taken, I posted the elaborate document analyzing his performance on top of countless other school papers on my refrigerator door. My husband and I looked it over together with high expectations, knowing from experience that our son was a fluent and highly skilled reader. However, our reactions to the test results were strikingly different—so different, in fact, that I can use them here to succinctly demonstrate the contrasting views of a traditional (i.e., positivist) parent and of a critical educator.

I looked the document over, trying to glean some big picture from its numerous bar graphs and technical labels, its charts of skills and subskills (and possibly subsubskills—who remembers?). There were numbers for everything, scores galore, and an obvious concern for comparing the performance of this *subject* (never this *child*) to others in comparable age levels and grades. For every score, the results offered a comparison to some national norm in a chart demonstrating graphically whether the subject was "ahead" or "behind" his peers. It was obvious pretty quickly that he'd outperformed the national average by far in every "subskill" save one. Looking more closely to see what my son had "excelled" at, I found *reading comprehension* and *vocabulary* among other things. Then, I looked to see which category he was "deficient" in and found *word recognition.* I laughed and laughed.

My husband's eye was also drawn to the "problem" in word recognition, but his response was a far cry from my laughter. After all, he is not in the business of critically analyzing prevailing educational practice. As I was laughing, he turned to me in chagrin and barked "Good grief! LOOK how far behind he is in that. Let's get him a tutor—*soon.*" I imagine that my husband's reaction would be nearly universal among concerned parents: "The test shows he can do x but not y; we better get him help with y."

But I too am a concerned parent, and like my husband, I love my son and worry about his welfare. How, then, could I laugh at a deficiency in something as serious as *word recognition*? The answer lies in the connections between positivism, pedagogy, and educational psychology.

BUT THE WHOLE *IS* GREATER THAN ITS PARTS

Positivism assumes, remember, that knowledge is an objective, quantifiable thing. As such, the whole can be broken down into parts, and the parts can be grouped and sequenced logically. Thus, if we want to teach *reading*, we figure out what reading consists of—what its parts are. Then we group those things (phonics, comprehension, vocabulary, word recognition, and so on), and we sequence lessons in every area. Of course, we must test every area, too, so that we know if a student lacks any subskill she needs to move forward. Here is the rationale for "failing" a student: if subskill *x* hasn't been learned, then the child won't be able to take on subskill *y*. Grade 3 curriculum must be mastered before grade 4 curriculum, or the lessons of grade 4 won't be possible.

And here is the reason my husband was so upset about my son's problem with the subskill of *word recognition*: how will our son be able to read next year's material if he's having trouble recognizing words this year?

Only being immersed in positivist assumptions for so long could make someone blind to the obvious fact that the test's diagnosis of my son's reading ability was patently ridiculous. No one—not the test analyzers, not my husband, not me, not my son or his teachers—had any question that my son was a skilled reader who had little or no trouble comprehending a wide variety of reading materials. In what bizarre sense could he possibly be deficient in *word recognition*? What exactly might that mean? What are we to think of test results that indicate a child can readily understand what he reads, but cannot recognize words? What kind of a "problem" is that? How do we fix a reader who isn't broken while he is actually reading?

We had every indication—including ones far beyond the test results—that my son could make sense of words shaped into sentences, of words appearing in some sensible context. Isn't that exactly what readers are able to do, and isn't that what matters? No, not in the positivist paradigm; not when there is an assumption that the appropriate approach to teaching is to break wholes into parts to be mastered in sequence. Unfortunately, most parts are meaningless out of context. Thus, children are taught the alphabet in senseless ways ("circle every A on this page") and given information about parts of speech outside of a useful context ("circle the verb in every sentence"). When a child asks why such tasks are necessary, or resists meaningless work, the adult pulls rank and says either "Because I said so" or "Because you'll need to know this later."

The first "later" that matters is test time. And since tests focus on the same senseless bits we teach, they become equally meaningless. In order to test some subskill, like word recognition, it must be separated out from other subskills and tested in isolation. Thus, the reading test tried to measure how well my son could recognize words standing alone, completely devoid of meaningful context. Never mind that the only place a reader needs this subskill is on a positivist reading test (or worksheet).

Think about it. Where in a reader's experience do single words appear completely decontextualized? *Entrance* appears on doors; *Men, too,* appears on door signs, often next to a graphic figure representing a man—and often next to another door with the word *Women* and a graphic symbol for a woman. *McDonald's* appears next to buildings with a clearly recognizable shape and decor; *peas* appears on cans with pictures of that vegetable. In fact, I learned to recognize the Italian words *uscita* (exit) and *gabinetto* (toilet) after I read them repeatedly on doors that I needed to find in Rome. We learn to recognize words from reading them; recognizing a word out of context is simply *not* a prerequisite for reading it *in* context. Nor, except on artificial tests, are we ever called on to do so.

Similar inanities occur in tests of "writing." Again and again, tests claim to measure a variety of subskills: vocabulary, usage, punctuation, grammar, organization, and so on. Often, based on things like forced choices between "he and I" or "him and me," or between "who" and "whom," students are diagnosed as being deficient in this or that skill and assigned "remediation." But when in the real process of writing is a writer forced to make such choices? Never, actually, because a writer who didn't want to make a mistake and wasn't sure of the difference would likely recast the sentence entirely or check relevant rules in a reference book. And since when has knowing the difference between nominative and objective case ensured that a student would be a "good" writer? Anyone who's ever read any quantity of student writing knows full well it's possible for writing to be grammatically precise and organizationally impeccable—and still dull as dishwater or incomprehensible as a political speech.

The whole of reading and of writing and of historical understanding and of mathematical and scientific understanding—the whole of any sophisticated skill or understanding—is *always* greater than the sum of its parts. This is not to say that subskills might not be involved; certainly after a student understands the big picture of reading and writing, he might find some information on phonics or punctuation useful. But the parts ought not to be mistaken for necessary antecedents to the whole. How could a golfer learn to keep her head down when swinging a club, for example, if she practiced looking down outside the context of a swing? It doesn't matter if she can keep her head down when she's standing in the locker room without a golf club; it matters if she can do it as she's swinging. Similarly, it doesn't matter to me if my son can recognize words out of context on some standardized tests; it matters if he can do it when he's reading. It also matters to me that he knows how and when to look up unfamiliar words in a dictionary—but that's "cheating" on the test. How odd. Maybe we should pass some sort of law against readers looking up words they don't know to stop such behavior?

Of course, in a hierarchy of experts, the credibility of those on top trumps that of those below, and an experience-based, commonsense argument isn't granted much validity. As a result, in recent years there has been a steadily increasing body of research, books, and articles seeking to discredit the positivist part-to-whole approach. There's far too much material to adequately summarize here—but then, that means that anyone wanting more detail won't need to look far. For example, Frank Smith's *Insult to Intelligence* (1986), a highly readable book that critiques a positivist approach to reading instruction in great detail, is one accessible place to begin. Smith is not a critical theorist, but his book supports critical arguments by persuasively demonstrating that commonsense and common experience discredit a part-to-whole approach. Another good starting point is John Mayher's award-winning book about language education (1990), which explores and challenges the traditional paradigm; its title, *Uncommon Sense*, pointedly notes that sense is something that has become very uncommon in education indeed.

Just how did so many senseless ideas and practices ever become such sacred elements of "the way things just *are*" in education? And what does all this have to do with Ed Psych 101 anyway?

ED PSYCH, INSTRUMENTAL RATIONALITY, AND ABSURDITY

In a positivist world, the quest is always toward certainty, and everything is hierarchical. The more one knows, the more expert one becomes, and the more power one has to lay out blueprints for others to follow. Always, the most expert is the researcher who knows everything in his specialized field and contributes new knowledge via research. So it has happened that the work of teachers has long been designed by experts from outside the classroom: historians, mathematicians, scientists—and, of course, educational psychologists and researchers.

What teachers do in classrooms is based on educational psychologists' ideas about how students learn and how best to make learning happen. Of course, once we start talking about "learning," we're back to the question central to the last chapter: "What exactly does it mean *to learn*?" And here's where the backdrop of positivism becomes increasingly noticeable.

For years, psychological researchers have considered the goals of school to be self-evident and clear—and thoroughly positivist: learning means acquiring and remembering information. How could they assume otherwise, since they were immersed in a cultural world framed by a positivist paradigm? Of course, information could be divided into its component parts; in fact, there was so much of it, it had to be. The questions of educational psychology centered for decades not on *what* to learn, but on *how* to ensure "learning," how to know when it occurred and what practices made it happen. This is why critical theorists describe traditional educational psychology as being focused on instrumental rationality. Researchers working from this perspective ask: "To reach the (unquestioned) goal of 'acquiring' knowledge, what procedures, or what instruments, are best?" Assuming that science can answer any question, they never doubt the validity of their stance: "If the question is rationally, objectively, logically researched, surely we can 'discover' universal procedures for teachers to follow." From this perspective, what is "good" is what "works"; what "works" is what best promotes retention of information. The "one best way" to attain high scores on post-tests became the field's Holy Grail. Evolution of the field has led to the idea that there might be a menu of best ways instead of a single best way—but the belief that specific teaching strategies can be researched and prescribed remains firmly in place.

Given the hierarchy generated by the positivist paradigm, it isn't hard to understand how this happened. Because education wanted very much to gain respectability in the university as a "real" science, it adopted the objective methods of natural science, even though anyone not blinded by unquestioned assumptions could plainly see that individual children behave with a great deal more variability than two chunks of carbon. Traditional educational psychology assumes not only a nonproblematic goal (helping children remember things), but also a homogeneity among children that is nothing less than absurd. While we manufacture a wide range of clothing sizes for their very different bodies, we maintain a "one-size-fits-all" attitude toward children's intellectual development. The unique experiences and information that children bring to classrooms are routinely treated as irrelevant in research on *how* teachers "should" teach (though anyone would laugh themselves silly at the thought that children with different body sizes ought to be made to wear the same size clothes, which some expert had decreed appropriate for their age). The child interested in writing is to be taught the same way as the child who fears it; the child who has a full library of books at home is to be taught the same way as the child whose home contains no books or magazines at all.

As natural scientists sought to define genus and species of plants and animals, educational psychologists worked to organize the stuff of the classroom, independent of the attributes that make children human rather than flora or fauna. They focused on determining which divisions of information, which sequencing of subskills, which practices and activities in the classroom would lead surely and directly to optimal "learning." What was "normal"? What was not? Since goals seemed obvious, assessment seemed obvious. "How will we know if they've learned? Why, we'll give them tests to measure recall and to monitor acquisition of subskills. We'll ensure mathematical reliability and validity of our results, and then we'll *know* who has learned how much of what. We'll be able to tell who needs instruction or remediation in what."

Just as one might count legs on a critter to classify it biologically, educators began counting the circles children made on standardized materials and tests in order to classify them educationally. Numbers came to outweigh sense and experience; if a test said a child had difficulty recognizing words, then the child had difficulty recognizing words, and his reading ability be damned. (Of course, this happened most often to poor children—but that's an observation I'll take up in the next chapter.) If an "expert" phonics text said children must learn *f* before *d*, then there could be no skipping ahead to *d*—and children had to be able to recognize *f* and *d* in isolation, even if they had no trouble reading the word "food" in a sentence.

All of this becomes a house of cards when we begin questioning base assumptions about what constitutes learning, what the goal of schooling ought to be, and whether it's possible (let alone desirable) to design effective practice without taking variability among children into consideration. If we agree with the alternative views that facts are inert until human consciousness imposes some sense on them, that learning is sense-making rather than retention, that it's silly at best to work from part-to-whole in the classroom, then what relevance can so much traditional educational psychology have?

It's as if expert technicians have designed for us the most fantastic airplane imaginable—but, since our goal is to get to the local supermarket, all their design expertise and the resulting product do us not one bit of good. To recycle a metaphor from the last chapter: a computer analysis can tell us all about mileage from Pennsylvania to New York, which roads offer the shortest route to Manhattan, and how long we can expect each leg of the trip to take—but all that information will be totally useless if our goal is not New York, but California, and if we're planning to fly rather than drive there.

THE PROBLEM WITH PIAGET

Because the work of Piaget is the foundation on which much current thinking in educational psychology is based, it's necessary to understand how Piagetian ideas have contributed to an educational world which is as insensitive to the uniqueness of individual human beings as was any Skinnerian experiment with rats.

When Piaget did his groundbreaking work on how humans process new information, he hypothesized that all learning involves either *assimilation*, finding a way to make new information fit into preexisting ideas about the subject or world, or *accommodation*, the ability to modify preexisting ideas so that new ones fit into the framework. As he explored how this process might work, however, he focused on identifying predictable stages of growth and concurrently assumed that the stages would follow each other linearly. That is, the framework of his research assumed that there are universal stages of intellectual growth, that each stage would be a prerequisite for the next, and that each new phase constituted a "step-up" toward some maximum achievement. The processes of accommodation and assimilation were triggered by a person's need for *equilibration*, a stable mental state where all contraries or inconsistencies seem resolved.

In the modest context of a single chapter on educational psychology, this is a necessary oversimplification of Piaget's work. Still, even this superficial sketch outlines areas that have led to rigid and limiting practices that run counter to the critical theorists' vision of a world of multiple perspectives, realities, and possibilities.

First, in pursuing a model of intellectual stages, Piaget assumes the positivist tenet that "teaching" is a matter of shepherding students through some predictable, universal sequence. In earlier, behaviorist manifestations, the sequence involved primarily bits of information; in Piagetian ones, the sequence involves different sorts of intellectual ability. But in either case, the uniqueness of every human student becomes irrelevant, and pedagogy is based on a one-description-fits-all model. Of course, there might be some slight variation in the age individual children reach different intellectual stages, but the *range* of ages and the sequence of growth is identifiable. Skinnerian theory might lead to one sort of classroom activity and Piagetian to quite another, but in either case there is no consideration of children as unique individuals with unique interests and talents. A teacher needs only to measure class members against Piaget's template, conduct instruction on the levels they're on, and try to move each child on to the next level.

The entire idea of moving forward, moving up, also reinforces the kind of hierarchy typical of positivist education. The focus is always on the next step, on more and more and more; more information in one case, more rungs on the developmental ladder in the other. Education becomes a game of more and more, faster and faster, getting from here to there as quickly as possible, being "ahead of " or "behind" others, "ahead of " or "behind" where one "should" be. And, at the end of the line is abstract thinking, the highest of all educational goods, the most advanced of all intellectual skills. The more a person can disconnect from the real world, the farther away one's thinking is from daily life's objects and experiences, the "smarter" one is in Piaget's terms.

Critical theory offers several challenges to such thinking. First, since every human being is inescapably shaped by such factors as where and when he was born, what values his parents held, how lucky he was or wasn't in opportunities to explore the world, what language he speaks—by a kaleidoscope of variable factors shifting differently for every human being—the critical theorist argues it is absurd to postulate some "pure" human developmental process. The idea that all humans experience the same sequential developmental process belongs in the realm of positivism, where it's assumed single "right" or "true" answers are possible. Instead, for the critical theorist, every answer is only one possible answer among many; every model, however useful, is only one possible model among many. And since each of us has a unique perspective on the world that is shaped by our surroundings, there is no way to factor a human's interaction with her environment out of any developmental process. Ignoring environmental influence ensures theoretical inadequacy.

Moreover, assigning abstract thinking a higher order seems a cultural decision rather than an "objective" one. Where is the stone handed down from on high proclaiming that people who can think outside of life experience are "smarter" than people who can weave strikingly beautiful blankets from raw materials? Who says abstract thinking should be prized and privileged? Such judgments come not from some god of education, but from the upper echelons of the highly educated. Interestingly, these are the same people who were nurtured in the culture that most uses and prizes abstract thinking; these are the same people who are themselves unusually talented in thinking abstractly; and these are the same people who design the models that tell others who is "smarter" than whom.

Why exactly should abstract thinking be more valued, more rewarded, more honored than other, real world talents? What of the artistic and musical ability of a Cassat and a Beethoven, for example? What of the ability to understand and inspire other people, of a Dr. Martin Luther King? What of the ability to visualize what modifications might make a set of house plans better suited to the needs of a specific family, as my uncle, a master carpenter, was easily and brilliantly able to do for me? What about the ability to make any child stop crying, which my father-in-law exhibited to a degree I've never seen in another human being? What kind of intelligence do these abilities depend on, and why are they of less value than the ability to think outside the world of people and things? Conversely, on a matter much closer to home: should I be required to give my doctorate back because last summer at the beach, after I bought a cheap puzzle book at the local newsstand, I spent two full days working out a logic puzzle only to formulate a wrong answer—twice?

Contemporary researchers are beginning to ask such questions and are beginning to formulate the kinds of varied answers that the critical theorist insists are possible (and that might allow me to keep my degree in good conscience). From Howard Gardner, for example, we hear about eight largely unrelated kinds of intelligence, including musical, spatial, bodily kinesthetic, and interpersonal. From Robert Sternberg, we hear about contextual intelligence. From Daniel Coleman, we hear about emotional intelligence.

When educational psychology manages to meander away from unquestioned assumptions about the value of abstract thinking and from traditional assumptions about what people need to learn and how they should learn it, a world of new opportunities opens up for the classroom practitioner—and a much more inclusive and inquisitive classroom climate develops. For example, I recently experienced a demonstration art appreciation class conducted by a professor who believes that the body can be useful in coming to "know" a work of art. Through a variety of exercises in which participants used their bodies to recreate the feeling or mood of paintings and sculptures, I personally came to understand a great deal more about art in one hour than I ever understood through several traditional college courses. And, my learning came about through a shift from logical thinking to metaphorical thinking, and through a shift from reason to emotion in my responses.

Like many of our cultural assumptions, the assumptions that have shaped educational psychology have led to an educational world limited by several fixed horizons. Given the influence of educational psychology over educational practice, in order to conceptualize and pursue a new kind of classroom, we will first have to challenge sacred ideas from Ed Psych 101 that steer practice into the same kinds of ruts, over and over and over again.

WHAT MIGHT A POST-FORMAL EDUCATIONAL PSYCHOLOGY LOOK LIKE?

If you're looking for *an* answer to the question above, you've not yet quite caught on to critical theory's emphasis on multiple possibilities. The only certainty is uncertainty and change. Still, having said that, there are certain characteristics we can anticipate in any manifestation of a psychology claiming a critical perspective.

A critical psychology will be based on a perspective that insists on the questioning of all assumptions and on the validity of multiple realities. Therefore, it will also be characteristically antithetical to traditional formalist psychologies and their fixed procedures, questions, and answers. While formalist psychologies assume that emotion and reason are incompatible, a critical psychology would assume instead that emotion and reason are simply alternative ways of knowing the world. Readers familiar with the old *Dragnet* television series may recognize the formalist perspective in Sergeant Friday's relentless insistence on "Just the facts, ma'am"—no feelings or speculation about the crime allowed. A Friday steeped in critical theory, on the other hand, might find the witness's emotional impression that the villain looked exactly like the devil as useful as knowing the criminal's exact height.

Viewing reason as only one tool we can use to know the world, a critical psychology will avoid the formalist's search for single, reliable understandings and instead seek multiple possibilities. Reason might tell Friday that *only* the wife had motive and opportunity to kill the husband, but intuition might repeatedly indict the butler, even if he had a strong alibi and even if only the wife's fingerprints appeared on the gun. How often has experience shown each of us the power of intuition to accomplish what reason could not? Surely we've all seen enough movies and read enough books to know that often the *only* person who seems reasonably and certainly innocent of the crime is the one who actually committed it. Why should we accept the word of "experts" that only reason is acceptable in our mental toolbox? And how do we evaluate such expert claims when we know that various government agencies sometimes employ psychics?

Readers who are "catching on" to the critical perspective may already see how a critical psychology will consciously shun formalist insistence on certainty and singularity. Unlike formalists, critical theorists deny that there is only one credible version of reality. Instead, they insist that to deepen our understanding of the world, we must learn to perceive from as many perspectives as possible. The deeper our understanding of the world, the better we'll be able to act consciously in it. Whereas formalist theories impose blinders on our view, postformalist theories lobby for broadening our horizons.

Believing that all wholes are greater than their parts, critical theorists argue that we need many other tools—music, art, emotion—to construct an informed vision. While too much emotion may distort our vision, so does the lack of any emotion at all. Humans are both rational and emotional, and reason should not be separated out from the human psyche as the most valuable part, as if it were nutmeat to be extracted from a worthless shell. A critical psychology will inform us about how we might implement the full range of tools at our disposal to explore the world in all its richness and diversity. The sterility of an exclusively rational approach will be replaced by a multifaceted vision more inclusive of humans in their totality.

In short, a postformal educational psychology would explore and value a wide range of mental tools for knowing the world, and it would pursue multiple versions of "reality." And here the traditionalist shudders: without prescribed methods of transmitting fixed information, without prescribed and standardized materials, what could a *school* possibly do and be? How could school *not* become an abyss where students would learn *nothing* because there was no agreed upon *something* for them all to learn? How could we be sure that anything they *might* learn would have any value? How in the world does a theory of multiple realities translate to specific classroom goals? And what kinds of things would teachers actually be *doing* in classrooms in this sort of educational world?

As radical and unrealistic as a critical approach may seem to many readers, the reality is that many of the ideas it embraces are hardly new. John Dewey argued long ago that education constitutes *miseducation* when it consists of memorizing and regurgitating meaningless bits of information:

> How many students, for example, were rendered callous to ideas, and how many lost the impetus to learn because of the way in which learning was experienced by them? How many acquired special skills by means of automatic drill so that their power of judgment and capacity to act intelligently in new situations was limited? How many came to associate the learning process with ennui and boredom? How many found what they did learn so foreign to the situations of life outside the school as to give them no power of control over the latter? (1938, 26–7)

Arguing against traditional, positivist education, Dewey anticipated that any alternative model of education might be challenged as empty—and his answer to such a challenge was simple:

> Just because traditional education [is] a matter of routine in which the plans and programs were handed down from the past, it does not follow that progressive education is a matter of planless improvisation. (28)

Dewey, of course, had all kinds of thoughts on what kinds of plans and goals were in order for schools, which he detailed in several volumes of work.

But the essential point here is that his plans shared critical theory's emphasis on the need for all citizens of a democracy to be equipped to think and act effectively within it. From this perspective, a school's primary goal must be to educate autonomous, empowered citizens who know they have choices and can analyze the choices they make. In pursuit of this goal, Dewey argued that "the conditions found in present experience should be used as sources of problems" in schools (79), and that, therefore, "a single course of studies . . . is out of the question" (78). Dewey's emphasis on participatory democracy and on multiple classroom procedures, basic as well to post-formalist thought, indicate that critical theory has roots reaching into the early nineteenth century, into the work of one of education's greatest theoreticians.

More contemporaneously, a current approach to the teaching of literature—commonly referred to as a *reader-response* approach—also embodies significant characteristics of critical goals and psychology. Here, too, we can identify the roots of current thinking in work done decades ago. Even the early writing of Louise Rosenblatt, which outlines a theoretical base for reader-response pedagogy, is replete with passages that might have been written by one of today's critical theorists. And interestingly, Rosenblatt herself had no trouble translating her theory of education into productive classroom practice—nor have the many writers and teachers who have followed her lead.

READER-RESPONSE THEORY AS CRITICAL PIONEERING

Like Dewey before her and the critical theorists who come after, Rosenblatt (1938) argued that when traditional, positivist methodology banishes the nonrational from the classroom, it actually diminishes students' intellectual ability:

> Perhaps adolescent students are often impervious to the appeal of literature because for them words do not represent keen sensuous, emotional, and intellectual perceptions. This indicates that throughout the entire course of their education, the element of personal insight and experience has been neglected for verbal abstractions.

Few teachers of English today would deny that the individual's ability to read and enjoy literature is the primary aim of literary study. In practice, however, this tends to be overshadowed by preoccupation with whatever can be systematically taught and tested. Or the English program becomes what can be easily justified to parents and administrators, whose own past English training has produced skepticism about the value of the study of literature. (50, 64)

Everything about traditional methodology de-emphasizes the personal and the experiential; Rosenblatt objected strenuously to such methodology largely because of its focus on texts (the "subject matter" of the course) and its parallel disregard of students' humanity. In opposition, she argued that if students were to learn anything of use in the literature classroom, their own experience and background had to be central concerns in any effective pedagogy:

The individual reader brings the pressure of his personality and needs to bear on the inextricably interwoven "human" and "formal" elements of the work. If his own experience of life has been limited, if his moral code is rigid and narrow or slack and undiscriminating, the quality of his response to literature will necessarily suffer. Conversely, any sensitivity to literature, any warm and enjoyable participation in the literary work, will necessarily involve the sensuous and emotional responsiveness, the human sympathies, of the reader. We shall not further the growth of literary discrimination by a training that concentrates on the so-called purely literary aspect. (51)

In short, if schools are to educate literate and perceptive readers, then the students—and not the material—must matter most. In traditional methodology, however, the nature of students has been completely ignored, often producing classroom conditions nothing short of bizarre:

During a reorganization of education on the Indian reservations some years ago, it was discovered that in some classes the Indian boys and girls were being required to read Restoration comedies. It seemed ridiculous that these children, whose past experience had been only the conditions of the reservation village and the vestiges of their native culture, should be plunged into reading the sophisticated products of a highly complex foreign country remote in space and time. Can it be doubted that the children could "make nothing of it"? Any show of "understanding" a Restoration play would undoubtedly be only a parroting of empty words and phrases to satisfy a teacher's demand.

The plight of these Indian children probably differs only in degree from the average American child's relation to much of the literature he reads in his classroom. (57)

By ignoring the fact that classrooms contain people as well as information, educators working within the formalist paradigms have created alien spaces for children who too often cannot survive, let alone thrive, in them.

Rosenblatt is particularly critical of such classrooms because she perceives the goal of literature study to be the nurturing of a critical and empowered citizenry. While she doesn't use the critical term empowerment (detailed in chapter eight), her concern for that goal is clear:

> Our schools and universities must be transformed, as C. S. Peirce said many years ago, from "institutions for teaching" into "institutions for learning." The student should go to school and college, not for the purpose of being taught ready-made formulas and fixed attitudes, but in order that he may develop the will to learn. . . . he must develop the flexibility of mind and temperament necessary for the translation of that sense of truth into actual behavior. Instead of judgments accepted in whole cloth, he must acquire a curiosity about the causes of human actions and social conditions; he must be ready to revise accepted hypotheses in the light of new information; he must learn where to turn for this information. He needs, in short, to develop a dynamic sense of life, a feeling that an understanding of causes makes for greater control of conditions. Instead of drifting with the stream of circumstance, he will be able to set up more rational personal and social goals and to understand better the conditions under which they can be achieved. (132)

> The aim, surely, is to enable the student to make intelligent judgments. . . . The question [of what we should teach] is this: Will this objective knowledge affect his actions, inside and outside the school today, and will it influence his actions in later adult life as a member of a family and as a member of a national and world community? . . . Democracy requires a body of citizens capable of making their own personal and social choices. The corollary of this is that they should be emotionally and intellectually aware of the possible alternatives from which to choose. (176, 193)

The purpose of any teaching, then (but especially the teaching of literature), must be to help students develop the intellectual and practical skills they need to become active, effective, fully literate citizens. Any educational methodology that forces students to uncritically absorb someone else's idea of what's important is antithetical to this democratic goal.

Rosenblatt also understood the need to combat hegemony in classrooms, though again the term was not in use at the time. She argued strenuously that students' emotional responses to literature could serve as an essential tool for helping them uncover their own unconscious, cultural assumptions.

> An undistorted vision of the work of art requires a consciousness of one's own preconceptions and prejudices concerning the situations presented in the work, in contrast to the basic attitudes toward life assumed in the text. . . . The reader's own reactions, like the work of art, are the organic expression not only of a particular individual but also of a particular cultural setting. . . .

> The attempt to work out the author's system of values and assumptions about man and society should enable the student to discover the unspoken assumptions behind his own judgment. His conclusions about this particular work imply the unarticulated theories of human conduct and ideas of the good that shape his thinking. . . . By bringing their own generalizations into the open, students may be led to feel the need of putting their mental houses in order. They will see how often they have been dominated by ideas only because they have heard them repeated again and again. They will develop a more critical, questioning attitude and will see the need of a more reasoned foundation for their thoughts and judgments, a more consistent system of values. (115, 118, 120)

By openly discussing their assumptions, by scrutinizing their sense of what is "good," students can learn to avoid a pitfall all too common in any society, the tendency:

> to accept the familiar or the traditional as possessing a fundamental rightness and, conversely, to consider the strange and the unfamiliar as necessarily inferior or reprehensible. Since the individual unconsciously absorbs the particular modes of behavior, views of human nature, and ideas about socio-economic arrangements, of the culture into which he is born, he takes them for granted and often cannot even imagine any possible alternatives or variations. Hence, when he does encounter another cultural pattern, as when the white man comes into contact with the African or the Samoan, he tends to look upon it as inferior. (157)

And after students learn to challenge their own unexamined assumptions? What then? Will they be left to wander, as opponents of critical theory charge, in a relativistic void, bereft of moral signposts? Not at all.

> Any system of values can be scrutinized in terms of its consequences for human life. Any form of conduct, any social mechanism, any custom or institution, should be measured in terms of its actual effect on the individual personalities that make up the society. To use the culturally sanctioned terminology, every human being is entitled to "life, liberty, and the pursuit of happiness." This means that the human being is

recognized as having value in himself and that anything which reduces him to the status of a thing, instrument, or automaton is condemned. . . . The corollary of this is that if a conflict of interest should arise, no individual or group would be justified in gaining their own satisfactions through exploitation of any other individuals or groups. (165, 166)

Implied here is the critical theorists' constant questioning of whose interests any prevailing value system serves, and what its costs are to others.

On multiple counts, then, Rosenblatt's work is an early version of current critical theory and critical psychology. It argues persuasively that schools ought to empower students for participatory democracy, that their emotions have a place in the classroom, that who they are as people must be a prime consideration in pedagogy, that multiple readings of a real world object are not only possible but essential, and that it is a prime concern of education to help students free themselves from paralyzing, hegemonic ideas.

What all this means in terms of classroom practice is outlined in *Literature as Exploration*, from which the above quotes came. Further explorations of classroom practice have also been fleshed out in countless works by other practitioners and theoreticians in the years since Rosenblatt's seminal work appeared. Today, countless secondary and university teachers use a reader-response pedagogy daily in classrooms nationwide. Scholarly, as well as pedagogical, work in the field has shown Rosenblatt's ideas to be educationally valuable and unquestionably practical, demonstrating that the vision of contemporary critical theorists is anything *but* radical, pie-in-the-sky educational thinking.

Still, few traditionalists will be eager to abandon the lessons of a positivist Ed Psych 101 and to embrace this new perspective, despite its venerable ancestry. Once we shift from one view to another, we won't be able to avoid confronting many other implied changes in day to day practice. Chief among these is an implied shift of power and privilege, both inside and outside the classroom. Why such a shift is both necessary and inevitable is the topic of the next chapter.

Chapter Five

RETHINKING AUTHORITY
Cultural Capital

The notion that intelligence is a personal endowment or personal attainment is the great conceit of the intellectual class, as that of the commercial class is that wealth is something which they personally have wrought and possess.

John Dewey

PRIVILEGE AND POWER

Authority in American society is both unequally distributed and easily recognized. People without power work in assembly lines, behind long counters at banks, or in large corporate rooms crowded with rows of desks. In contrast, people with power work in spacious, private offices, usually with someone stationed outside to control access to the plush inner sanctum. Authoritative teachers and professors sit on one side of a desk, compliant students on the other.

According to popular American rhetoric, those issuing directives from plush sanctuaries are in their positions because they've proven themselves more worthy than others. They've earned good educations, confirming their intelligence. If they have large salaries and bank accounts, it's because they worked hard to earn them. The wealthiest and most powerful among us are generally assumed to be our smartest and most hard-working citizens.

For many of America's affluent, that description fits. Many of the wealthy are impressively intelligent and amazingly hard-working, and everyone has heard about whiz kids like Bill Gates who have taken ideas and built financial empires upon them. But critical theory reminds us that there is always more than one story if we look for it; there is always more than one reality in any human experience. While it's no doubt true that many have made fortunes in America by virtue of their hard work and wit, it's also true that others have acquired their authoritative positions by far different means. Specifically, critical theory suggests that while some people earn their positions by virtue of what they do, others acquire their positions by virtue of what they have. That is, they are equipped with cultural capital (a term taken from the work of French sociologist Pierre Bourdieu), a resource that nets them privileged positions, regardless of how much intelligence and ambition they may have—or lack. Cultural capital includes a variety of components that readers will surely recognize in the discussion that appears later in this chapter.

As a prelude to that discussion, however, I will detail a personal experience in order to demonstrate not only what cultural capital is, but also how it operates to privilege some over others. It's possible that the tale will trigger unhappy memories of similar experiences for many readers, memories of times when others judged them and found them wanting. Or, conversely, perhaps others will read the narrative and begin to wonder if they have ever mistaken the benefits of their own cultural capital for evidence of their own superiority.

In either case, rethinking our own experiences may be distinctly uncomfortable. It's worth the effort, however, because such honest analysis can yield an intensely personal understanding of how privilege is sometimes purchased, rather than earned. And, in a culture that assumes that we all get what we deserve, such understanding is useful both for those who have power and for those who lack it.

THE RIGHT STUFF

Many years ago, I sat across a mahogany desk from a middle-aged man in his office, the president's office of a college preparatory school catering to children of the moneyed. Every aspect of the office reflected that fact: plush carpeting, hushed ivory walls, original artwork, windows overlooking a flowering manicured campus. I was there, I told him, to find out why I was fired—or rather, in the euphemistic language appropriate to the environment, why my contract was not renewed.

I watched the flush rise from his crisply starched, brilliant-white cotton collar up past his scholarly spectacles and through his thinning, impeccably groomed hair. With barely controlled fury at the audacity that allowed me to think I had a right to require an explanation of him, he gave me a tight, tidy answer: "Because," he spat at me, "people like you are a dime a dozen."

People like me?

According to student evaluations, I was a talented, caring, and creative teacher. Students and parents alike had launched a campaign for me to chaperon the school's annual summer tour to Europe. I had stacks of notes from students praising my work. I had spent countless Friday nights shepherding students safely through ski trips with drunken bus drivers, and countless Saturday nights preventing female boarding students from climbing out their windows to visit the boys' dorm. But—having never even looked at my classroom, one floor above us, in the three years I'd been teaching there—this man wasn't thinking about my work.

He meant that I grew up in a local town on the wrong side of the tracks. He meant that my degrees were not from Ivy League schools. He meant that my long blond hair was not subject weekly to the ministrations of a stylist favored by fashionable local women. He meant that my name had too many syllables, and it had consonant combinations that were unfamiliar to him, and I was not Protestant.

I knew what he meant because I had already learned it as a teenager working as a "mother's helper" in homes where I was routinely referred to as "the girl" and expected to eat alone in the kitchen. And, in one memorable case, to iron the father's boxer shorts.

Of course, no administrator could possibly fire a teacher for having the wrong sort of name and hairstyle. Something else must have happened; of course it did. But the specific triggering event only magnifies how little success and failure, power and powerlessness, can be related to intelligence and hard work, and how much they can depend on far different standards.

BOBBY

I was fired because of Bobby, and I have never for a second regretted it. Decades later, in fact, when I studied with the superbly humane philosopher Maxine Greene, I realized that if I hadn't gotten myself fired I would have had to be ashamed of myself for the rest of my life.

Bobby was a sophomore when I met him. He was resident smart-aleck in one of my classes, ring leader of the class clowns in a class overflowing with comic talent and seriously short on intellectual curiosity and energy. He made my life miserable, and he sent me scurrying to every book I could find on group dynamics to figure out how to turn around the insurgent class climate he orchestrated. The books were no help.

To make a very long story short, Bobby and I became friends when we started encountering each other every weekend in the dormitory where I had an apartment. When I was on duty, monitoring the dorm, I spent a lot of time reading in the lounge, where students could drop by with questions on school work, or on whether they could leave, or on how to deal with life's habitual roller coasters. Though he lived nearby, at home with his mother, I soon learned Bobby spent all the time he could at the school, and it wasn't because of love of learning. His divorced mother was an alcoholic who abused him emotionally and verbally, and he counted every minute away from home a happy one.

As our hours of conversation mounted, the trust level between us grew, and we learned we had things in common. He, like me, was not in the same social class as the vast majority of the students. He was, in fact, a "scholarship student," one of the handful of kids the school supported to demonstrate its non-elitism. (I myself had been hired not through a regular application process, but as an emergency mid-year replacement for an unexpected retirement; I was certainly qualified, and so the school accepted me—not having time to seek someone qualified *and* "suitable.") His suicidal thoughts were familiar to me because, when I was younger, I had spent many hours in a dark room listening to music wishing my life would just go away and leave me alone. We became, eventually, friends and allies.

When I suggested to him that he start earning As instead of Ds and Fs in my class, he agreed to try, and exceeded even my high expectations. In class, he herded his buddies into interesting conversations with me instead of against me. When I suggested to him that he try earning As in his other classes as well, he did. In fact, when the school decided to kick him out, he was a straight A student.

But he showed up on campus drunk. Once. And the administration needed to make an example of someone—and Bobby suited their purpose just fine.

Student drinking, in a school where teens carried wallets stuffed with twenties, was a serious problem. Hoping to alleviate the situation, the administration had been waiting to find the right student to sacrifice in order to make a point about consequences. They caught John, but his father was a big contributor, and the same with Jane and others. But Bobby? No money there; no name revered in local halls of commerce or in our newspaper's social pages; not likely to become a big name, a big buck contributor down the road. So they nailed him, and sent his case—that of the obviously ungrateful ne'er-do-well—to the campus disciplinary board.

Which is how I got in trouble. I personally visited and pleaded ardently with every member of the board, "Not *this* boy, please. Not THIS boy." It will, I told them, ruin him. It will, I told them, undo months and months and months of rehabilitative effort on my part and Bobby's part. It will, I told them, waste precious human potential.

But they kicked him out anyway.

And I descended upon the dean in a fury, charging him with hypocrisy and ethical cowardice. And the episode made clear to the authorities that I was, alas, a troublemaker who didn't know how to go along to get along. And, after enough time had passed, I was fired.

But, six months after *his* dismissal, Bobby was in a mental institution.

WHAT BOBBY AND I LACKED

For twelve years of schooling, every morning students proclaim a belief that America is about "liberty and justice for all." As I've noted, we learn early that America is a meritocracy, where people get what they have earned. If they work hard, they get money or grow up to be president of something, maybe even the country. If they're lazy, then they become poor and lead spare lives of hardship because they don't have the ambition, or maybe intelligence, to make their lives better. In any case: whatever they've got, it's what they deserve.

However pervasive this popular wisdom (and however comfortable for the privileged to believe), the critical theorist urges us to rethink it. If we look at the issue of who has what from a different angle, we uncover considerable validity in another saying, popular in other quarters: "Them what has, gets." Maybe Bobby and I deserved our fate; but then again, maybe other factors came into play.

CULTURAL CAPITAL

Critical theorists suggest that the assortment of characteristics they refer to as cultural capital—including but decidedly not limited to towering bank accounts—enables some people (like the school president and the disciplinary board members) to attain certain positions and the power to determine the fate of other people (like Bobby and me). The theorists suggest that often we are sorted into groups-with-power and groups-without-power based not on how smart we are or how hard we work, but on very different characteristics: how we look, speak, and move; what we already do and don't know; what we do and don't value; where we go and don't go; whom we know or don't know. Having a certain constellation of characteristics, a certain cultural capital, enables holders of the "right stuff" to acquire power, while lacking it shuts others out of the ranks of the powerful.

For example, when the president said that people like me were a dime a dozen, he meant that few people held his sort of cultural capital, the "right" sort—Ivy League degrees, a moneyed background, a pricey wardrobe, the ability to chat about restaurants in cities from coast to coast. Many, however, shared my cultural capital—degrees from local colleges, knowing how to juggle bills so that there would be enough money to pay the rent, skill in making eight mix-and-match pieces of clothing do as a wardrobe, the modest idea that going for pizza constitutes having dinner out. When the disciplinary board dismissed Bobby, they chose him because other students had cultural capital which he lacked: the right name, the right street address, the right financial resources, the connections to assure him of a lucrative job after college.

Have one set of cultural capital, and it buys you power. Have one of countless other sets, and it persuades the powerful that they have the right to determine your fate—that you deserve no more than you've got already. I still believe that Bobby and I were removed from the school because we lacked the right cultural capital. We lacked the proper credentials to belong, really, and those credentials had nothing to do with our intelligence, ambition, or ability (he was earning As, after all, and I was earning praise from students and parents). And, to compound my lack of appropriate cultural capital, I clearly didn't know my place. I told anyone who would listen that Bobby was being punished not for drinking, but for being different from the majority of his schoolmates in all the wrong ways.

School authorities looked at us both and shook their heads: "Here are these impostors, lucky enough to dwell among us, and yet they don't know enough to count their blessings and just follow along, quietly. There's just nothing you can do with *some* people." Except, of course, exile them: send them back to where they belong.

OUR CULTURAL TEMPLATE

Momentarily, I'll get to greater detail on which cultural capital is valued in schools. But first, it's worth asking how and why we accept such a sorting system in the first place, consciously or not. After all, anyone can have a good idea no matter what clothes he might be wearing, no matter what her language or dialect. So why do we value one particular set of characteristics over others? Why should wearing this kind of clothing or that, speaking this way or that, determine whether we are to wield power or to suffer the power of others?

The answer is that as a culture, we have tacitly endorsed a particular template as representing the "average American," and that template has become our ideal, the "right" way to look, and sound, and live. We have absorbed an ideal so pervasive in our culture that it has become simply a part of *the way things are*, something we never stop to think about or to question. Thanks to positivism and religion and science and mass media and a historic sense of moral superiority, we are a culture that believes (as many other cultures do) that we alone have identified the one *right* way to live, to speak, to act, to believe. Anyone who doesn't fit what's represented as the norm doesn't belong. Anyone who varies lacks "the right stuff " and belongs in the group without power.

Theoretically, it is the job of schools to make sure that students have the stuff they need to be successful. As discussed in chapter one, the goal of American schools has long been to function as a melting pot, erasing differences among individuals by processing them in the mold of standardized public schooling, involving not only academics but *Americanization*. "This is what *Americans* eat; this is how they sound; this is what they wear; this is what they value." Anything else is un-American and, since this is the greatest nation in the world, inferior.

So strong is our commitment to the rightness of our vision that we have all but wiped Native American culture from the face of the earth. And, in another spectacle of national hubris, we once forced Puerto Rican schools to celebrate American holidays and Puerto Rican teachers to teach Spanish-speaking Puerto Rican children in English. Even if you're not living in America, we think you'll be a lot better off if you act more "American" than whatever you are.

The template of "an American," however, is taken from images far removed from the daily experience of the majority of American families, and the public school has never been able to erase what are largely characteristics of class. While June Cleaver was wearing pearls to putter in the kitchen, my own mother was sloshing around my dad's dairy in her knee-high rubber boots. My grandmother spoke only Polish until she died, despite Walter Cronkite's nightly English intonations, and every Sunday I suffered through two homilies at church, one in Polish and then one in English. While the "average American" was reading the stock reports in daily newspapers, my Irish father-in-law was spending his nights studying accounting with a generous nun, who shared his hope that he would one day own the warehouse floors he spent his days sweeping. I never read about or saw pictured in my textbooks anyone mentally challenged, but all the kids in my hometown knew that the ever-visible Crazy Louie was someone who would not hurt us and who deserved courteous treatment.

In other families and areas, less fortunate than the homey neighborhood of extended families where I grew up, children routinely wore hand-me-downs and went to bed hungry. They lived crowded into one-room hovels. They saw their fathers, who worked impossibly long hours in mines or in fields, almost never. Nor did they see much of their mothers, who scrubbed other people's floors or laundry all day, and who were likely to have left school after the first few grades to help their families by picking cotton or coal.

Most "average" Americans have never lived the lifestyle portrayed as "average" in our newspapers, magazines, textbooks, or television shows. Still, that is the way we are "supposed" to be. (Many novels, like Stephen Crane's *Maggie, A Girl of the Streets*, have painted a different picture, of course—but such books are rarely urged upon the "average" American.) Public images of neat women wearing pearls, men in suits behind desks, well-scrubbed apple-cheeked children, and rooms of coordinated, pristine furniture (never, of course, draped in plastic or polyester for protection) have effectively obscured the more commonplace and less attractive reality. That reality—that a whole lot more of us live far differently than the image presented as typical—is as true today as it was when I was young.

In the butcher shop in the New York neighborhood where my dad's family once lived, young and old butchers and customers alike still converse more often in Polish than in their heavily accented English, and pigs' feet are still prominently displayed in the meat case. In other areas of the city, newer generations of immigrants speak in a cacophony of assorted Asian and Pacific languages. I know plenty of people who have trouble paying the rent on minimal housing, never mind mortgages on individual spacious homes.

Men disappear from their homes, tired of telling dependent wives and children that they didn't find jobs again today. Single mothers work multiple jobs trying to support their children, left home alone with the mother's most ardent wishes that it could be otherwise. For decades, educational researcher and activist Jonathan Kozol has been documenting the immoral and apparently eternal suffering of countless American children living in poverty for countless reasons. Any of his works thoroughly discredits the myth of a universally happy and innocent American childhood. Meanwhile, despite volumes of evidence to the contrary, recent politicians like Dan Quayle and Newt Gingrich have stubbornly denied the documented, ugly reality and worked to maintain the fiction of a two-parent, hard-working, financially stable family as the core American experience.

The people who live and work and dream in America, including the children, rarely resemble the popular myths about them. And, the reality is that while all of America's schoolchildren come with plenty of capital from their own culture (with lilting phrases in foreign languages, with games and songs from non-Christian religions, with an enthusiasm for traditional foods bearing no resemblance to turkey, with unique ways of deferring to or of challenging adults), children who don't reflect the standard cultural template pay a heavy price for their uniqueness. In schools, they are judged on multiple markers having nothing to do with their intellectual capacity, and they are routinely found wanting.

The critical theorist calls attention to the fact that what is wanting are certain kinds of cultural traits, or cultural capital, rather than intelligence, creativity, or potential. Among these are mastery of standard English, accumulation of privileged knowledge, and patterns of interacting.

ISSUES OF LANGUAGE

Though I don't remember what prompted the incident, I do remember being in seventh grade and running into Miss Williams's room with some friends, all of us bursting to tell her the most exciting news *ever*. Breathless, we clamored "Miss Williams, Miss Williams! You won't believe this! You should of been there. . . . " As our news started pouring from us in our grinning excitement, she interrupted with a stern admonition: "Girls, please: You mean should *have*, not should *of*." We left soon after, her impromptu grammar lesson having pricked the balloon of our passion.

In large part because positivists have *a* right answer to everything, the focus of much teaching is to find the places where children are *wrong*, or deficient, and to fix them—to pinch and pull and tug at them until they more closely resemble the national template. In the area of language, this effort is very nearly obsessional. The *form* of a child's remark routinely outranks, by far, its content.

Lucy Calkins, specialist in the teaching of writing to children, frequently tells an anecdote that poignantly reveals this teacherly disposition. She shows audiences of teachers a piece of writing from a child, telling about his grandfather's death. The text is full of errors—sentence fragments, spelling, punctuation—all the errors that make English teachers grind their teeth. When Calkins asks teachers where they would start in responding to the writing, teachers usually fiercely dispute whether it's best to start with sentence errors (the most "serious") error, or to start with spelling, arguably the easiest to correct. When the teachers finish planning their grammatical crusade against the child, Calkins quietly notes that she herself might respond, "I'm very sorry to hear your grandfather died. It's obvious you loved him very much."

It's true, of course, that at this moment it is necessary to master standard English to attain status in American society. Anyone who says in an interview "I ain't afraid of hard work" is unlikely to be hired for anything except brute or rote work, no matter their intelligence, their ambition, or their eagerness to excel and advance. In our national template, the use of standard English is generally thought to signify intelligence. Speak the "right" way, and you are deemed smart enough to enjoy responsibility; speak any other, and you are deemed stupid and pushed back to the bottom rung of the ladder, where you obviously belong. A current national obsession to proclaim English the official language of the United States and to outlaw bilingual education speaks volumes about this perception.

So does standardized testing, where being able to discriminate between *who* and *whom*, and *which* and *that* is thought to signal whether or not one is smart enough to go on to college. This perception is absurd, of course, since most of us learn our speech patterns from our parents and others who surround us as we grow. By the time she was five, for example, my daughter had learned to say on occasion that her brother had "soggy drawers." Because this was a favorite phrase of mine, I never misread her parroting as genius; I never confused her linguistic experience with her intelligence, though that is a habit of the educational world. There, however, the misinterpretation is more likely to suggest idiocy than genius: if a child doesn't sound like the teacher, he or she is thought to be stupid.

However much anyone may believe that smarter people use "more correct" English, most linguists will tell anyone who will listen that *no* language or dialect is inherently superior to any other. *Any* language form people continue to use is adequate, because its continued use indicates that it meets the needs of the speakers. There's nothing *wrong* with saying "I ain't"—unless one is measuring against some ideal template. It's an *alternative* way of expressing an idea, not a useless corruption. The National Council of Teachers of English endorsed this position in the 1970s, and reformers like linguist Geneva Smitherman are actively campaigning to advance respect for alternative language styles.

This is not, however, a position endorsed by most teachers (and most power holders). In a positivist environment, the focus is on doing things the one *right* way, not on alternative ways of seeing and doing, not on the variety of legitimate perspectives that constructivists endorse. There are countless Miss Williamses to signal to children they are wrong, wrong, wrong, wrong, *wrong* nearly every time they open their mouths. Because they are corrected—told they fall short of an ideal—over and over, they soon learn an effective strategy for avoiding this humiliating judgmental process: silence. They learn to keep quiet, knowing that the teacher isn't listening to their *ideas* anyway. And then, of course, their silence marks them as lacking ideas, being dim-witted or slow. It's a lose/lose proposition for the child.

Many will protest, as student teachers I worked with did, that it *is* the job of the school to teach standard English, so that children can gain acceptance in mainstream (read prosperous) America. This is true, and it explains why standard English is sometimes referred to as "cash English" in some cynical circles. But, as I told the student teachers repeatedly, there is a difference between teaching a "standard" version of a language and a "correct" version of a language. A "standard" is a form we all agree to in order to facilitate living.

Because there are "standard" size windows, architects can draw plans without checking over and over and over again on what window manufacturers are doing these days. Because in the United States the standard of road measurement is miles rather than kilometers, we can drive from state to state and read signs that offer us useful information in a consistent format. (Though soon, we will be moving to the metric system in order to bring our idiosyncratic measurements in line with a more global standard.) Because we have "standard" English, outside my region I know I can use the phrases "Isn't it?" or "Don't you agree?" as tag questions and have a listener understand my intent—unlikely if I used our alternative regional term "haina?"

Standard English is, no doubt, useful—but that's all it is. Useful, not sacred. Many educators, linguists in particular, plead with purists to consider what it is they are requiring of children forbidden to speak the language of their homes. In asking children to master a new, *correct* speech form, we ask them to accept that their home speech, the speech of their mothers and grandmothers and fathers and neighbors, is inferior. We ask them to accept that important people, people in their cultural world, talk *wrong*. They sound stupid. In short, we ask children to stop sounding like members of the community they call home and to start sounding like members of a hypothetical middle class white world. Instead of sounding like, and so identifying themselves with, their mothers and grandmothers, they are asked to sound like, and identify with, the teacher (whom they may not even like or respect or believe), or the guy who reads the Wall Street report on the evening news.

Critical theorists call attention to what children are asked to sacrifice and to their frequently resulting silence. Rather than suffer correction after correction, each yet another sign of deficiency and inferiority, children often choose to distance themselves from their schooling in order to maintain their identities in their home communities. As constructivists who believe in multiple realities, many critical theorists argue that this needn't be an either/or situation.

They say, "Let's call standard English what it is: cultural capital. Let's admit that it buys things in this society— jobs, higher education, respect. But let's also honor the unique language of the home community and let the teacher learn about the student's home language while the student learns about the standard. Meanwhile, let's try to move toward a society where we enjoy our diversity rather than scorn it, where the society pays more attention to the message a speaker offers than to its form."

PRIVILEGED KNOWLEDGE

When I applied to the college I eventually attended, it was because my father gave me two choices, and two choices only. He would pay, he said, for a local college because its higher tuition would be offset by my living at home. Or, I could go to a state university, where the lower tuition meant he could afford room and board. I was the first member of my family to attend college; what did any of us know about how to make this critical decision? The local college wasn't famous, but it *was* a good, and expensive, one. The state university was widely respected. We knew I'd get a good education at either place. Why look beyond those two choices?

I got my first clue about our miscalculation years later, when the school president pointed out my "dime a dozen" status. And my learning about academic elitism eventually culminated when I earned an Ivy League doctorate and saw how differently my job applications were greeted, how differently I am now perceived and treated. I am the same person, I think, just as intelligent and just as hard working as I was when I held two degrees from a non-Ivy school—but my doctorate has a sort of halo that seems to outshine other doctorates from other institutions.

For all our talk about anyone being able to do anything, American society is terribly elitist, and an enormous part of that elitism is enabled by academic snobbery. Knowing the difference between applying to colleges like Wellesley or Amherst and to "Hometown College" is a privileged piece of information, held primarily by people who have attended schools like the former. In fact, even when I decided to pursue a doctorate, I still was unfamiliar with the names of truly prestigious institutions. I learned the name of the impressive school I eventually earned my degree from only when my intensely supportive dean—whose own doctorate was from Yale—suggested it to me.

Overworked guidance counselors, whose job it is to know the difference and to help students make choices based on ability, routinely fail to mention high status colleges and universities to students of a certain background, on the theory that they "can't afford them, anyway." As a result, many capable students, not knowing the difference, apply to community colleges (if they apply to college at all) because they don't know they could do otherwise, or what ultimate difference their choice might make in the future. Meanwhile, students at pricey private schools (sent there primarily by parents who themselves went to similar schools) receive an extensive education about premier institutions and how to get into them.

It may be true that "You can get a good education anyplace," definitely including thousands of quality community colleges, but the reality is that a degree constitutes a kind of cultural capital, and a degree from one place will "buy" the holder a great deal more than a degree from someplace else. Given the hegemony of America's privileged, most of America's young people either don't know the relationship between colleges and the opportunities that they will or won't encounter later, or else their constructed consciousness keeps them from applying to elite schools on the grounds they know they don't belong there. In this self-selecting process, young people as smart as any Ivy League graduate deny themselves a chance to compete for high status. They lack privileged information about elite institutions and the advantages they confer.

Similarly, many of my students don't know that they have rights as citizens. For example, I routinely require students to attend school board meetings, and when I make the assignment they frequently ask "Are we *allowed*?" Here, too, constructed consciousness tells them they don't belong, they have no voice, the business of governing is not properly a concern of theirs. Oh, yes, of course, they know they have the right to vote, but no one has ever explained to them the relationship between campaign money and political success, or how letter-writing or boycotting or demonstrating might affect political decisions. No one has urged them to have a political memory beyond the seven days preceding election day. Despite twelve years of pledging allegiance to the flag, they don't understand American government; they don't *know* in any real way why and how they might work to influence politics and political decisions.

Because the experience of many students is so different from that assumed in our national template, there are countless pieces of privileged knowledge they don't have, and so countless opportunities for others to judge them stupid and unworthy. They don't know that every human being deserves respectful treatment from others, whatever their sex or job or bank account may be. They don't know how to invest money to make money, or how to minimize the taxes they pay. They don't know that their permission is required for actions schools may want to take in relation to their children, or that they have every right to walk into a public school classroom and ask a teacher questions about how a child has been treated.

Because they don't move in certain circles, there's a lot they don't know. Their ignorance is neither bliss, nor a sign of stupidity. Instead, it is a form of blindness imposed by their class status that keeps them from acting on their own behalf or even misleads them into acting against their own best interest. When it comes to information about accessing institutions that confer privilege and power, what many people don't know—their lack of a certain kind of cultural information—can and does hurt them.

PATTERNS OF INTERACTING

When I taught graduate school in New York City, I was privileged to make friends with several African-American students who weren't offended by my nearly total ignorance of their culture. (At the time, I still suffered from a positivist hangover and hadn't yet begun studying other cultures in earnest.) Instead of scorning my ignorance, they undertook my education.

I learned from them that if a tall, young black man happens to be walking toward a single white person on a sidewalk, the white person invariably crosses to the other side of the street. White people also shy away from groups of loud, laughing young blacks. The simple traits of height, age, race, and volume are routinely interpreted by whites to be threatening, to signal an inclination to perpetrate violence. My towering male friends were both saddened and angered by this perception, but they could do nothing about their height and they didn't see that sounding more subdued, more like the white template and less like their cultural selves, made much sense.

I also learned an important cultural lesson from a Korean woman I once had in a writing class. Though she had a lovely, delicate oral style in English, she felt her written English needed to be more "correct." Because this event also happened when I was still influenced by a positivist perspective, I looked at her writing and agreed it needed improvement. Subsequently, I set about trying to teach her what a thesis is and how paragraphs support a thesis by providing support for a single idea, how writing stays focused.

No matter how much time we both invested, however, her essays remained long rambling tracts without any sign that she was making progress toward tightly woven exposition. At least I had the good sense at the time not to confuse her rambling with stupidity. I knew she was intelligent because of my conversations with her, but something certainly seemed to be getting in the way of her understanding my instruction.

Too late, I learned that what I perceived as "rambling" served in her culture as courtesy. The directness I was asking for, the sharply focused, clearly supported ideas, was for her the cultural equivalent of telling someone to "Shut up!" rather than asking "May I have a moment to tell you how it looks to me, please?" Cushioning a sharp remark with blunted language is, in fact, typical of Asian culture. In Amy Tan's *The Hundred Secret Senses*, for example, a character from a relatively privileged background teaches a character from much poorer circumstances that the equivalent of "Mind your own business!" in polite Chinese is "In this matter you need not concern yourself on my behalf."

Because courtesy was one of the most prized virtues in my Korean student's culture, my directions to "Get to the point!" equated to asking her to sound like a rude and ignorant oaf—though of course I mistakenly read her continually roundabout discourse to mean she was unable to comprehend my instruction. To compound the problem, she had no way of telling me what I was asking of her: criticizing or complaining to an instructor would constitute another act of unconscionable rudeness on her part. Instead, she politely and quietly accepted my idiotic and endless repetition of the same advice, which was to do something her culture would soundly condemn.

Children from cultures other than the theoretical mainstream often come with habits that are misread by their teachers, just as I erred in the case above. Our misreadings are nearly the equivalent of judging the taste of French bouillabaisse by how closely it resembles American beef stew. Different ingredients and intentions need to be interpreted differently, but we rarely take care to discriminate so thoughtfully among student behaviors.

Teachers often have a menu of desirable traits they judge all students by. Boys should be outspoken, energetic, irrepressible within bounds, smudged and rumpled, but not smelly. Girls should be modest, reticent, generous, neat, and squeaky clean. All children should follow directions without question, be dedicated to any schoolwork presented, and eager to answer the teacher's questions. All children should also profess love for their parents, country, school, and God. They should be able to look the teacher in the eye, and they should promptly volunteer in any area the teacher requests. Ad infinitum.

The trouble is, as is true with standard English and as I unwittingly asked of my Korean student, the behavior a teacher expects, or even demands, may be directly in conflict with behaviors valued or forbidden in a student's home culture. In *Ways with Words* (1983), for example, Shirley Brice Heath explains how children from a certain culture did badly in their English class because they appeared to lack any imagination. Asked to write "a story," they resorted over and over again to well-worn Biblical tales. To the educational world, the children gave every indication of lacking any shred of imagination, perhaps because they were "culturally deprived."

When Heath studied the community, however, she found it a deeply religious one that stressed both honesty and faith to the literal word of God, found in the Bible. As tots, the children memorized "stories" from the Bible, giving great care to being able to repeat them exactly, word for word—an ability highly prized in their community. Their religion taught them that dishonesty was unacceptable under any circumstances, and frowned on fiction as a form of untruth. As a result, the children were paralyzed when in school they were asked to write "stories," which to them constituted a form of lying. Instead, they offered the behavior prized by adults at home, and repeated the Bible stories they'd taken such care to learn verbatim. And the school misread their obedience to a strong, highly principled home community as lack of imagination—dullness.

This letter from an unidentified Native American mother to her child's American schoolteacher, quoted by William Ayers in *To Teach* (1993), poignantly demonstrates how a mismatch in cultural values may cause children to be devalued in schools:

Too many teachers, unfortunately, seem to see their role as rescuer. My child does not need to be rescued; he does not consider being Indian a misfortune. He has a culture, probably older than yours; he has meaningful values.

He is not accustomed to having to ask permission to do the ordinary things that are part of normal living. He is seldom forbidden to do anything; more usually the consequences of an action are explained to him, and he is allowed to decide for himself whether or not to act.

He has been taught, by precept, that courtesy is an essential part of human conduct and rudeness is any action that makes another person feel stupid or foolish. Do not mistake his patient courtesy for indifference or passivity.

He doesn't speak standard English, but he is in no way "linguistically handicapped." . . . He and the other Indian children communicate very well, both among themselves and with other Indians. They speak "functional" English, very effectively augmented by their fluency in the silent language, the subtle, unspoken communication of facial expressions, gestures, body movement, and the use of personal space.

You will be well advised to remember that our children are skillful interpreters of the silent language. They will know your feelings and attitudes with unerring precision, no matter how carefully you arrange your smile or modulate your voice. They will learn in your classroom, because children learn involuntarily. What they learn will depend on you.

Will he learn that his sense of his own value and dignity is valid, or will he learn that he must forever be apologetic and "trying harder" because he isn't white? Can you help him acquire the intellectual skills he needs without at the same time imposing your values on top of those he already has? (40-41)

With good reason, many mothers, like this one, fear that their children will be misunderstood and misjudged by their teachers. While they may not use this vocabulary to express their fear, they are in fact worrying that the cultural capital their children take to school, like knowledge of the Bible or of different ways of communicating, will be discounted, while their lack of privileged cultural capital, like knowledge of behaviors the teacher expects and values, will lead authorities to judge them innately inferior.

CULTURAL CAPITAL AND THE SORTING MACHINE

Because it is the job of schools to identify and nurture various levels and kinds of talent among children, schools have nearly countless sorting practices: grades, ability groups, tracks, ranges of test scores, report card grades. Theoretically, children receive the grades and placements they have "earned" by virtue of their ability and application. The reality, however, is far different. Their particular cultural background has far more to do with how children fare in schools than does their ability.

The next chapter, on how children are sorted unfairly and on how they resist sorting, explores the relationship between cultural capital and the fate of students in America's public schools.

Chapter Six

RETHINKING AGENDAS
Social Reproduction and Resistance

I wouldn't cooperate in the remaking of myself. I played the dumb
Indian. They couldn't make me into an apple—red outside and white
inside.

Lame Deer

A THEORETICAL MERITOCRACY

Education is widely touted as the way to get ahead in American society.
From the moment they enter school, children are told that it is necessary to
do well in school in order to do well in life. Teachers talk about students
"making something of themselves," of "becoming somebody" as a result
of their school work. Students hear over and over that if they work hard,
do well, get a good education, then success—most often interpreted as a
bulging paycheck—will follow as surely as night follows day. High grades
are a form of pay for this preliminary work, low grades a kind of
punishment for the unambitious, or a reality check for the unintelligent. In
either case, grades foreshadow what students can later expect
economically: "No work/no brains, no pay."

This perspective on education is central to America's faith that its
citizens occupy their particular economic and social slots because those
slots are what they *deserve*, what they have earned when given a chance to
prove their worth. Public schools are supposed to offer everyone an equal
opportunity to prove themselves and to monitor educational competition
carefully to see who shows ambition and talent and who doesn't. If
everyone has equal educational opportunity, then the American race for
power and status is fair, and the losers have no cause to complain.
Theoretically, the winners who eventually attain wealth and power *earn*

them by demonstrating superiority in the classroom; the losers who achieve less status *deserve* less, because they failed to excel when given the chance in school.

The belief that a fair competition occurs in schools helps keep our democracy operating reasonably peacefully, despite its stunning discrepancies in wealth and privilege. How can the poor rebel when they've been given a fair chance to better their lives and failed? What more can citizens reasonably ask for than a fair chance to compete for the gold ring? If a person's lot isn't a happy or prosperous or powerful one, whom can he blame for his fate but himself?

The scenario sounds fair and reasonable, says the critical theorist, but it often bears little resemblance to the lived reality of many students. Rather than serving to give nonprivileged students a genuine opportunity to do better than their parents, schools far more often serve as a mechanism to keep students in whatever class they started out in. It's a fairly intricate but essentially circular process, like the mazes in which a ball is released into a series of chutes and gadgets, and then goes up, down, and around—only to mysteriously return exactly where it began. And there it begins again, repeating the process over and over, despite all of the intricate interventions en route. In critical theory, this process is known as "social reproduction": the schools' tendency to take students in, to run them through a variety of placements, evaluations, and coursework—only to deposit them years later in precisely the same social class where they began.

Of course, since we can't count on fooling all of the people all of the time, long before their release from school many students realize that, for them, the educational process is a maze leading nowhere rather than a fair race. With this realization, their relation to the school may become strained. When students come to believe that they are being judged on qualities other than intelligence and ambition, when they lose faith in the educational sorting system or in the rewards it promises them, they often refuse to continue playing the game.

In such cases, students find a variety of ways to reject the system and all of its components, a reaction critical theorists call "resistance." Resistance is the equivalent of getting up and walking away from the card table when you've figured out that the other guy has stacked the deck. Unfortunately, the result remains the same: while students can't win a rigged game, they also can't win if they don't play. Educational inequity is a lose/lose situation for disadvantaged students.

After discussing both "social reproduction" and "resistance" in more detail, I'll share a real life example of exactly how they can undermine the potential of a gifted student. The example comes from a videotape that is available from PBS, one that (as I'll say again later) I'd urge readers to see for themselves.

FLAWED SORTING MECHANISMS: STANDARDIZED TESTING

My own experience provides the most telling example I can imagine to demonstrate the many problems that exist with standardized testing, one of the most common and most powerful sorting strategies schools use to monitor the educational race and divide students into groups of winners and losers.

Needing to pass a language test for my doctorate, which I was trying to complete while working full time in one city and maintaining a family life in another nearly three hours away, I decided to be pragmatic. I'd studied Spanish for years in college, but hadn't done anything with it for well over a decade. I couldn't help wondering if it was remotely possible that I would remember enough to pass a language exam. Rather than spend time studying if I didn't have to, I eventually decided to take the test without any preparation, a calculated risk. If I passed, wonderful; then I would save time I could spend on other work. If I didn't pass, it would cost me only another $20 to take the test again, because there was no academic penalty for failure. At test time, I knew I was in big trouble as soon as I opened my booklet. The first half of the exam was on fine points of Spanish grammar and usage, the equivalent of English tests forcing a choice between *who* and *whom*. An accent over the *i* in one word made the word *yes*; no accent, and the word became *if*. That I knew, but I was clueless on most of the others. I had no chance of passing this portion of the test based on what I remembered of my Spanish classes, for sure.

Of course, what I *did* know a lot about was standardized testing, having tutored many high school students on the SATs. I knew about when to guess and when not to guess, and I knew a lot about how tests were scored. I also knew how many points my department considered a passing score (interestingly, "passing" scores varied from department to department). Since there was no point in my thinking about Spanish grammar as I sat there, I analyzed the test statistically instead, groping for some strategy to eke out enough points to pass.

I mentally wagered that I'd do much better in the second part, involving reading comprehension. I estimated that I could get nearly two-thirds of the comprehension questions right, and calculated how many points I could earn there. Then, estimating that I'd answer no more than one in four grammar questions correctly, I calculated how many questions in that section I'd need to attempt in order to have a prayer of earning the points I needed.

I answered exactly the number of grammar questions I thought I *had* to, carefully selecting those that I felt I had the best chance of guessing correctly. And, I was immensely relieved to find later that I did indeed understand the reading passages pretty well, even the memorable one on sarcophagi. (Now there's a word every doctoral student needs to be able to identify in a foreign language!)

And, I passed the test—literally by a point or two. But what, exactly, did my passing score signify?

If being successful on the test was supposed to demonstrate industriousness, I should have failed; my only preparation had been reading Spanish signs at the Miami Zoo. If being successful was supposed to demonstrate that I knew the finest points of the most formal use of the language, I should have failed. I didn't *know*; I *guessed*. I had little of the knowledge that half the test targeted.

But I didn't fail. And, I would argue, I should *not* have failed, because what I did know was more important than what I didn't. I *did* have sufficient command of the language to be able to read original texts in it, which seems to me a primary skill for a researcher. Certainly being able to read in the language ought to have mattered more than being able to identify a linguistic faux pas equivalent to using *who* instead of *whom* (especially since I wasn't allowed access to a reference book; do test makers imagine that researchers work without dictionaries and other references at hand?).

The test, however, focused equally on faux pas and comprehension, suggesting they were equally important. The result is that even though I could make sense of a text far removed from my own specialty (sarcophagi are about as far removed as one can get from English education), I *would* not have passed without my extensive understanding of the structure and grading of standardized, multiple choice tests. My passing score depended not on my knowledge of Spanish grammar and spelling, but on privileged knowledge about testing I had because of my background—because of my cultural capital. As I often say to my students when I tell them this story: "Go figure. Who can say what my test scores *meant*, really?"

Here, in the nutshell of this one experience, are all the reasons that the standardized tests so often used to slot children into gifted or "special" classes, or into academic or vocational tracks, are untrustworthy. As most teachers know (even if statisticians refuse to believe it), standardized tests often do not measure what they are said to measure. And, what the tests do measure is often of little consequence, except to people obsessed with grammatical purity, or with *the* answer *they* think is right. What sense does it make, really, to think that a student who knows the difference between *among* and *between* is smarter or more able than one who doesn't? And, what talents remain hidden when tests ignore student knowledge that is actually more important than material on a test? For example, wouldn't it have been useful for my professors to know whether, left to my own devices with a dictionary and handbook, I could write a reasonably correct sentence in Spanish? Surely that's a more important skill than how well I can guess where an accent mark belongs in a sentence written by someone else.

As if these problems weren't enough to discourage standardized testing, many researchers have noted that students may lack cultural knowledge that a test presumes, as when students don't understand the form or impact of standardized tests, or when urban elementary students are asked a question related to the structure of a "porch," or rural students a question related to a "stoop."

So many examples of stupid testing abound that it's somewhat mystifying why the educational establishment continues to rely on them. Well, that's disingenuous on my part. Many of us know that how much it *costs* to administer a given test will determine whether it's used or not. We use the test formats and the information that are easiest and cheapest to administer, even if results are likely useless or misleading. Generally, educators and testing agencies are much more interested in the *appearance* of being rigorous than in gaining useful information.

For example, another test idiocy I am familiar with comes from the experience of a friend who teaches high school English in New Jersey. She was so dismayed at the form of a much ballyhooed "new and improved" state writing test that she conducted her own research to demonstrate that what was being tested was *not* what the test makers claimed (Coyle 1992). Specifically, one section of the test was said to measure students' "revision" skills. In this section, students responded to multiple choice questions requiring them to "revise" targeted sentences using one of four options provided. As the teacher's research demonstrated, the test reveals little about students' actual revision skills.

For starters, never in the real world does anyone revise a sentence targeted by someone else, using one of four options designed by someone else. It's a tad difficult to imagine a situation in which a boss might say: "Bill, I really like what you've drafted here, but I think you should revise this sentence in one of these four ways. Of course, three of these options are wrong, so you better know your grammar and usage." Where is the sense of this format?

Another problem was that most of the questions focus on the same sort of silly editing problems that I faced in my Spanish test, more *who/whom* equivalents. Most English teachers have long since agreed that such choices are editing problems (simple rule-based problems) rather than revision problems (significant problems involving content and organization). Solutions to editing problems can be found in dictionaries and handbooks; solutions to revision problems must be designed by the writer and an infinity of solutions are possible. Still, test makers continue to design tests suggesting that getting a comma in the right place is the ultimate test of effective writing.

And, test conditions forbidding the use of dictionaries and other references routinely imply that in the real world no one will ever look anything up or ask someone more knowledgeable for help. I can't help wondering if these test writing folks work in some special vacuum where no one ever calls across a room—as they do everywhere else in my experience—"Hey! How do you spell *accommodation*?"

Finally, there are an infinite number of ways to shape any idea into written language; when left to their own devices, students demonstrated that they were likely to correct problems using far more sophisticated options than those provided. In fact, because the test makers' "correct" answers were so often awkward, students frequently rejected them on the reasonable grounds that they "sounded funny."

On the whole, this section of the state test shows only how well students can guess how test makers think, *not* how well they themselves can revise. It is impossible to imagine a multiple choice test that would reveal anything about students' true revision skills because there is *never* a single appropriate revision response to any text with a weakness. But rather than explore other, more appropriate—and certainly more expensive—assessments, authorities settle for a cheaper option actually focused on editing. The results can be reported authoritatively to the public—accuracy and usefulness be damned. Another prompt from a state test I've critiqued gives students five minutes to write a letter to a fictional character from a story they read the day before. In the story, the character dies of exposure in a cold climate. The students (who live in a somewhat southern state) are required to write a letter offering the (fictional) character (who is already dead) advice on how to stay alive in extreme cold. Immediately *following* this exercise, they read an informative article on hypothermia. Think about it.

Anyone who checks assessment literature will soon discover that researchers have provided copious critiques and arguments about the discrepancies between what standardized tests may *claim* to assess and what they actually *do* assess. Some of the most exemplary work has been done by Clifford Hill, a linguist who has clearly and thoroughly documented problems in a test widely used with children entering elementary school, and in some state tests as well. As Hill's work (a mere drop in the ocean of critical literature) persuasively indicates, not only are test questions often impossibly skewed by the test maker's perspective, but variations in students' linguistic and cultural backgrounds influence results in several ways that have nothing to do with intelligence or ability.

Is the test taker well-versed in test-taking strategies? Practiced in taking standardized tests? Or, if the test is written in English, is the student fluent in English and so able to understand the problems posed? Is the student familiar with the cultural experiences and vocabulary necessary to make sense of reading passages? If the student applies information from a different culture, does a different answer become logical? What about environmental influences the student can't control? Has she had a good night's sleep and a good breakfast? Does she understand, or believe, that this test will affect her future? To what extent, in short, might numerous experiential variables affect test results?

No matter what magical mathematical formulas statisticians apply to standardized tests, the tests themselves are devised and taken by live human beings who do not come from standardized molds. One test maker defines reading this way, another that way, and voilà! We have two entirely different reading tests claiming to measure precisely the same thing.

From a positivist paradigm, standardized, one-right-answer tests may make sense; the only need is to figure out which test is right and reliable and which is wrong and unreliable. From a constructivist perspective, however, where all of experience is open to multiple interpretations, such efforts at measurement fall little short of absurdity. They might, in fact, be amusing, if certain groups of students weren't routinely sorted into the same slots over and over again based on standardized test results, which many educators, parents, and politicians take very seriously indeed.

However much faith many profess in standardized tests, more than one educational researcher has reviewed results and noted, credibly, that—given the correlation between family income and standardized test scores—we might as well skip the expensive testing process and just assign students places based on their financial status right from the beginning. That, at least, would be more honest, if no more fair.

FLAWED SORTING MECHANISMS:
LANGUAGE, RACE, GENDER

As I explained in the last chapter, students who come to school lacking a command of standard English lack a kind of cultural capital that costs them a great deal in schools. If English is not their first language, they may receive academic instruction in a language they cannot fully comprehend. This means that they are introduced to unfamiliar concepts, like division, in unfamiliar language, making it doubly difficult for them to comprehend new content in subject areas. Or, they might be grouped into an ESL math class—where the teacher covers material more slowly, in light of their linguistic difficulties. But in either case, children whose first language is not English are slowed down while native English speakers forge ahead. Unfortunately, it is far more likely that their falling behind will be interpreted as an indication of lesser intelligence, rather than the consequence of not receiving instruction in their native language.

The above is intended as a realistic portrayal of the consequences of English-only instruction, not a dismissal of the many arguments favoring it, or of the very real financial and staffing constraints that preclude other arrangements. Bilingual education is a serious and complex issue, but a discussion of its pros and cons is beyond the scope of this text. Still, it is relevant to note here the fact that a student who begins elementary school without mastery of English does not compete on a level playing field with native English speakers.

Even for those who do speak English, however, language can be a handicapping issue. Dialects that vary from standard English, or unfamiliar cultural speech habits, may signal inferiority to a teacher steeped in the cultural notion of what a smart person sounds and acts like. The use of "ain't," as I've noted, generally triggers the thought that the speaker is stupid, for example, and loudness is routinely thought to signal aggression. So culturally ingrained is the latter perception, in fact, that young visitors to my home have fled behind their mothers' skirts in terror at my husband's booming greeting. Because he and three brothers competed as children for their mother's attention, loudness early became a speech habit for all four men. Children, especially children with no siblings, routinely find his normal speaking voice threateningly loud, and his brothers report similar experiences. And, it is a rare teacher who will not have a negative reaction to a student he perceives as aggressive.

Such preconceptions about language and voice carry over into evaluation of written work as well. A piece using the phrase "should have" is likely to receive a higher grade than the one using "should of," even if the latter has more impressive content. (It is, after all, so much easier to diagnose errors than weakness in reasoning.) Always, student performance is judged against the idealized cultural template of what "an American" sounds like, and routinely, students are evaluated academically based on the surface form of their thoughts, rather than on the intelligence or creativity of their content.

Caucasians, as well as other racial groups, suffer such language discrimination, but non-white races are likely to suffer from other forms of prejudice as well: "Everybody knows Asians are good at math; everybody knows African-Americans and Mexican-Americans just aren't, well, as intelligent or ambitious as some other folks." However much we would like to think that racism is over, the facts suggest it is not. For example, the recently best-selling argument for the inherent inferiority of African-Americans, *The Bell Curve* (Hernstein 1994), is prime, recent testimony that many continue to insist on the inherent inferiority of non-Caucasian races. Many whites claim that academic standards will fall when African-Americans begin attending a given school, and often standards *do* fall—to the dismay of parents seeking rigorous schooling for their children. Research has indicated that many teachers and administrators start easing standards and expectations downward when the population changes, based on their assumptions about what children who look or sound a certain way will be interested in or capable of. While there are, of course, schools where racism does not play itself out in lesser expectations and evaluations for African-American or Mexican-American children, there are countless schools where that is exactly what happens. Knowing that students rise and fall to teachers' expectations, we also know that any first grade teacher who looks at a racially mixed class and expects from Day One that one group of students will do better than some other group is also slanting the level playing field children are assumed to compete on.

Gender, too, can put half the population of any school at a disadvantage from their earliest experiences, as extensive research sponsored by the American Association of University Women has demonstrated. Reports of subtle and not-so-subtle discrimination against females is well documented in that organization's publications *Shortchanging Girls, Shortchanging America* (1991), and *Hostile Hallways* (1993), and in research reported by David and the late Myra Sadker (1994). The cultural template that urges girls to passivity puts them at a disadvantage in a classroom where boys aggressively seek the teacher's attention. The notion that boys are better at math and science than girls by nature leads again to lowered teacher expectations and lowered performance. And, sexual harassment of girls lessens their comfort and self-confidence in school, although it is often overlooked on the "Boys will be boys!" principle. Moreover, the typical school administrative structure, in which a powerful man heads up a staff of women who do little more than follow instructions, teaches females by example that they are to be followers rather than leaders.

Of course I am painting these areas with tremendously broad brush strokes that do not apply to every teacher or every school. Still, copious amounts of research verify that the biases and preconceptions I've described do directly affect the fate of students in schools.

By far, African-American, Mexican-American, and Native American students are assigned to less challenging courses. I am, of course, painting the situation with tremendously broad brush strokes that do not apply to every teacher or every school. Still, copious amounts of research verify that the biases and preconceptions work to channel specific groups of student into vocational courses of study. By far, wealthy students are given more and better counseling and preparation for higher education than poorer students. By far, boys outnumber girls in advanced math and science classes and in math and science professions as well. It is no accident, in view of all this, that men in American society still hold, by far, a greater number of powerful positions and earn, by far, larger salaries than women. *Some* men, some Caucasians, and some wealthy folk are surely more able than *some* women, some non-Caucasians, and some poorer folk. But consistency in comparisons, when analyzed in light of documented prejudicial conditions in schools, indicates that at least *some* people are where they are because the game was fixed in their favor, not because they competed hardest and best.

FLAWED SORTING MECHANISMS: *SAVAGE INEQUALITIES*

The term "savage inequalities" was coined by Jonathan Kozol, cited earlier as a researcher documenting the educational fate of poor children. His book by that name provides over 200 pages of evidence that the way we finance our public schools systematically ensures that poor children will *not* receive the same educational opportunities that middle-class and wealthy students do. Under the circumstances, it is virtually impossible for poor children as a group to compete with children from wealthier homes.

Kozol documents conditions in several geographic areas, showing the link between tax base and school conditions. Because school funding depends largely on property taxes, schools in areas with high property values—generally enclaves of the affluent—routinely have nearly unlimited resources. Meanwhile, essentially next door, schools in areas with low property values routinely lack funds even for such essentials as repairing broken windows or purchasing pencils and paper. For example, Kozol reports that before court rulings mandated change, a low-income city near Los Angeles was spending $595 for each student, while nearby Beverly Hills was spending $1,244 per student—despite the fact that residents of the low-income area were taxed at double the rate of the Beverly Hills residents.

The idea that education will never provide a level playing field until schools are funded more equitably has not been widely endorsed nationwide, despite America's constant prattle about equal opportunity. For example, even in California, where the courts mandated a more equitable system, the result was for voters to pass the legislation known as Proposition 13, which restricted funding for *all* schools. As a result of voter reaction to the court mandate, California's financial support for its public schools dropped to become one of the lowest in the nation, even as residents in affluent areas uncovered creative ways to channel extra money into their schools, merely restructuring the inequities the courts intended to outlaw. And, of course, children of the privileged can always be sent to well-endowed private schools, a luxury the poor have no way to access.

In chapter after chapter, Kozol documents conditions poor children endure as a result of inequitable financing that middle-class parents wouldn't tolerate for a moment. For example, Kozol reports that in Chicago on an average morning, 5,700 children in 190 classrooms have no teachers; in one school, eighth-graders work from a text that names Richard Nixon president; two working bathrooms that serve 700 children are short on soap, paper towels, and toilet paper because funds are short. In Camden, N.J., children learn typing on manual machines that their parents also used, a school fire alarm has been dysfunctional for 20 years, and there are *no* books for the ninth-grade English class. In Cincinnati, the single instructor for the remedial reading program sees 45 children per day; four computers serve a total school population of 600; nearly two-thirds of the school's current population can be expected to become high school dropouts.

And, in an East St. Louis school, raw sewage routinely floods the bathrooms and kitchen, as it does homes in the area, because the municipality lacks funds to repair its sewage system. Science labs are 30 to 50 years old and have no water. In winter, the eternally malfunctioning heating system turns classrooms into sweltering boxes with temperatures in the 100s. Texts, as in many schools, are scarce. Children routinely come to school suffering physical damage from exposure to grounds contaminated with arsenic, mercury, and lead. They talk casually about a specific site near the school where someone's young sister was raped, then murdered.

And, they know where they are and what is happening to them. The following words happen to come from children in Camden, but in Kozol's text, similar words echo over and over from children nationwide:

"I have a friend," says Jezebel, who is in the eleventh grade. "She goes to school in Cherry Hill. I go to her house and I compare the work she's doing with the work I'm doing. Each class at her school in Cherry Hill, they have the books they're s'posed to have for their grade level. Here, I'm in eleventh grade. I take American history. I have an eighth-grade book. So I have to ask, 'Well, are they three years smarter? Am I stupid?' But it's not like that at all. Because we're kids like they are. We're no different. And, you know, there are *smart* people here. But then, you know, they have that money goin' to their schools. They have a nice *clean* school to go to. They have carpets on the floors and air-conditioned rooms and brand-new books. Their old books, when they're done with them, they ship them here to us."

"Look at this." She hands me a paperback volume with no cover and with pages falling out. "You see this book? We have to read Charles Dickens. That's the book they gave me. Pages are missing. *A Tale of Two Cities.* We don't even have enough for every student. There are just ten students in that class! . . . Why are we treated like this?" (152, 154)

Another child asks Kozol similar, poignant questions:

"You visit other schools. Do you think the children in this school are getting what we'd get in a nice section of St. Louis?"
I note that we are in a different state and city.
"Are we citizens of East St. Louis or America?" she asks. (30)

Another tells of being the only black student in a fifth-grade class at a white school, of being taunted by the other students:

To tell the truth, it left a sadness in my heart. Now you hear them sayin' on TV, 'What's the matter with these colored people? Don't they care about their children's education?' But my mother did the best for me she knew. It was not my mother's fault that I was not accepted by those people. (35)

"It does not take long," notes this student's classmate, "for little kids to learn they are not wanted." That lesson—that society is indifferent to the fate of poor children—is evident in every facet of the alternately sweltering and freezing, understaffed and undersupplied, dirty and unrepaired schools Kozol describes. It is amazing to me—and to my students, and to Kozol himself, I think—that although this book has been available since 1991, there has been no outraged response insisting that we *must* remedy this national shame of inequity, and we *must* do it *now.* So disturbed was one of my students by this text that she bought copies and mailed them to Bill and Hillary Clinton, with an eloquent plea for their attention. But nothing seems to make anything happen.

In a conversation with Bill Moyers on PBS, educator Mike Rose, who specializes in teaching writing to the "underprepared" college student, talked about the injustice of the educational sorting system that routinely discriminates against large groups of intelligent and creative human beings. He argued, on the one hand, that justice demands that schools change the way they do business. But he also noted, with a good bit of historical evidence to support his point, that it is both foolish and dangerous for comfortable America to continue ignoring the fate of poor children.

What can we expect to happen when young people learn that a fraudulent story of America, Land of Opportunity, has been systematically fed to them? What will happen when they realize what the children in Kozol's book seem to have realized when they were still very young indeed?

RESISTANCE

Riots and looting in Los Angeles after the Rodney King verdict, as well as earlier riots in other places, have demonstrated what can happen when the disadvantaged come to believe that they have been systematically lied to and cheated by the society they inhabit. While some may continue to suffer in silence, others will choose more active responses to their circumstances.

Critical theorists suggest that when students realize that they do not in fact receive the equal educational opportunity America brags about, a common response is to resist what they are offered, to refuse to cooperate in any way with whatever seems expected of them. Of course, many teachers who still believe in the myth of equal opportunity cannot understand resistant behaviors, which often strike the adults as inexplicably bizarre.

Why, teachers wonder, do so many students dye their hair purple or green or blue? Or shave it off entirely? Why do they dress in leather, in feathers, in skin-clinging spandex, in pounds and pounds of jewelry—sometimes including even safety pins and pacifiers? Why do they pierce eyebrows, navels, noses, and tongues as well as ears? Why do they say *up* whenever a teacher says *down*? Why do they use every possible combination of profanities in the classroom, even in direct address to teachers? Why are they frequently destructive, breaking this and setting fire to that? That is, why do students do all this when they actually *come* to school? And how do we explain all those students who won't come, the ones who play football outside the schoolroom window as their class proceeds on the other side of the glass (as a friend teaching on an Arizona reservation recently reported to me about her students)?

Of course, some of this is the perennial need of youth to rebel. But critical theory suggests that much of it has a far more subtle and more worrisome cause. Such refusal to play along, such defiance and insistence on maintaining an identity clearly different from the one the school would impose, is what critical theorists term resistance. Resistance embodies the idea—surely novel to many educators—that students might choose to refuse to be remade in the teacher's image, to insist on maintaining their own integrity and dignity, to refuse to agree that their native culture and selves are inherently inferior. Students embracing this stance conclude that if the price of "success" is to look, sound, and act *white*, and middle-class white at that, then the price is too high. The concept of resistance does much to answer teachers' befuddled, wailing questions "But *why* do they have to look like that? *Why* do they have to talk like that? *Why* won't they cooperate and do what I ask? *Why* don't they care about their grades, about getting an education?"

Critical theory suggests that often, the only way students can maintain their self-respect is to refuse to endorse the premises that American schools embody: that there is *a* way for Americans to dress, move, and talk; that only the knowledge the teacher thinks is important matters; that there are right answers to everything, and teachers are the only ones who know for sure what they are; that if they allow the schools to remake them, and if they work very hard while they're cooperating, then they are sure to achieve whatever goal they pursue. "Play the game we offer you," schooling suggests, "and you'll win—if you're worthy."

But many students need only look around their neighborhoods to know what a lie these premises constitute. People of all shapes and sizes, speaking in all sorts of languages and ways, embody dignity and intelligence and creativity—so it must not be true that *only* if you look and sound a certain way can you be an admirable human being. Moreover, people willing to work hard, who may have gotten high school diplomas, are everywhere unemployed, or working for wages too low to support a family in dignity or comfort.

Glass walls and ceilings surround disadvantaged students and everyone they know, and students learn quickly that their schools are no more substantive than cardboard props. It's revealing, in fact, that many *poor* schools post multiple copies of the poster bearing the legend: " I know I'm somebody because God don't make no junk." Apparently, the posters are needed to counteract the message that poor children are nobodies, as the shabby provisions made for them in schools imply. Any meaningful learning that happens inside schools in poor areas too often happens not because society is intent on providing equal educational opportunity, but because there are good human beings to be found everywhere, and the ones who work in poor schools are at times nearly saint-like in caring for their students, in overcrowded and neglected surroundings, with few or no supplies.

Those students who lose faith in schools may remain in them anyway—because the law requires it, or because everybody has to be somewhere, and school is a place where a youngster can be sure of having a lot of company. But being there physically does not require being there mentally, and being disruptive can, from a certain perspective, equate with being honest in the context of a fraudulent system. Like Lame Deer, who refused to be made into an "apple" (red on the outside and white on the inside), and like many African-Americans who refuse to be made into what they term "oreo cookies," many students simply refuse to renounce the cultural identity they inherited at birth. Their acting out in classrooms is often the equivalent of someone angrily trying to knock over a card table after realizing the dealer has been using a marked deck—while telling the losers what lousy card players they are ("Anyone who works hard enough will succeed—so you people must not have worked hard enough or been smart enough").

Given these circumstances, I have long since stopped wondering why a student would choose to derail classes and to ensure his or her own failure in school. Now, instead I wonder at and admire the number of students who hang on, trying to be loyal to their families and cultures and to attain mainstream success at the same time. It can't be easy, as the following example demonstrates.

A VIDEO CASE STUDY

A video aired as part of a Bill Moyers program on PBS (1992) that compared the experience of two New York City students offers a startlingly clear example of how the inequities in school financing cheat poor students of opportunity and produce resentment and resistance among young people. Produced by a small group of New York City high school graduates, the video compares the experience of Lonnie, a student at South Fordham in the Bronx, with the experience of James, a student in the nearby, more comfortable area of Riverdale, during their first year in new, upper-level schools. Both schools are in the same district, only a few miles apart geographically, but because of differences in their tax bases, they have widely disparate resources.

James's school is clean and boasts well-groomed, outdoor sports areas in addition to an after-school community center where children are welcome to gather and socialize when classes end. Teachers in the school are certified in the subjects they teach, and in James's science lab, there is a microscope for every student. Students interested in music have the opportunity to play in a fully equipped band, with instruments ranging from trombones to flutes. Asked about their plans for the future, James and his friends talk about Ivy League institutions like Columbia, Harvard, and Yale. They talk of becoming professionals, and James's goal, to become a veterinarian, remains constant throughout the school year.

Lonnie's school, on the other hand, has far fewer resources. A cramped gym hosts several games at one time and is not available to the students for after-school recreation. A young man, whose qualifications are primarily that he has taught dance and swimming, teaches Lonnie's science class. With a shout, he urges the class to try to behave "like human beings for a change" when they talk among themselves instead of engaging in class activities. Specifically, students are not interested in the "experiments" conducted in this class with no equipment: climbing up and down on their chairs, checking the effect of the activity on their pulse, and lifting their notebooks to gauge the effect of nonstrenuous activity on their muscles. Few teachers are certified in the subjects they teach, and few have appropriate equipment to work with. The music teacher has not an assortment of band instruments, but minimal keyboards, to offer students.

In this environment, Lonnie—who, in elementary school, was an honor student in advanced classes—soon loses interest in schoolwork. Although he begins the year talking about becoming a lawyer, by mid-year his mother is sitting in on his English class to monitor his classroom behavior, and he falls into serious trouble in his science class. He becomes sullen and uncooperative. In a year-end meeting, Lonnie's mother tells the guidance counselor that Lonnie is bright and that he is bored with the work he's been given. In response, the disbelieving and patronizing counselor tells Lonnie that his grades offer no evidence that work he's been given is too easy for him.

In conversation at the video's end, Lonnie talks defiantly not of being a lawyer, but of being a basketball player. He tells his mother he won't return to the school, and when she says he must because they can't afford to move, he discusses the futility of time spent there: "What am I gonna learn in that science class?" he asks, knowing full well that in nearby schools students are receiving instruction from well-qualified teachers in well-equipped laboratories. Despite his mother's interest and support, despite his own intelligence and ambition, Lonnie's fate seems predetermined. He insists that he *could* be a lawyer, that he's smart enough to do the work it would take, but that he'll never get the chance because of the incredibly weak education his school can offer him. His mother notes, "He's right. If we stay here, he's *not* gonna make it." Even with straight-As, a student leaving his high school will never be equipped to compete with students leaving James's school.

Anyone who *believes* that America offers *all* of its children an equal opportunity to achieve their dreams needs to *see* this video (*Listening to America with Bill Moyers: Unequal Education*). Together with Kozol's *Savage Inequalities*, it offers incontrovertible evidence that much of the American faith in education as the great equalizer is sadly misplaced, that schools are far more effective at social reproduction than they are at equal opportunity. Together, the video and text also make it startlingly clear why students might choose to exhibit resistance—to reject schooling as fraudulent in its claim to be the path to a better life.

WHAT'S A TEACHER TO DO?

Surely, many teachers *intend* school to offer disadvantaged students an opportunity to attain a brighter future. In fact, many teachers work tirelessly, hoping that their efforts will help students attain their dreams.

What critical theory suggests, however, is that because the current system works so well to the *dis*advantage of so many students, working within the framework of the accepted system is not only futile, but even harmful. Efforts aligned with the current framework, however well-intentioned, nevertheless enable an ongoing and inequitable fraud.

What students *need* to change their life circumstances, argues the critical theorist, is *not* the factoids of standardized tests, but an understanding of their circumstances, of the forces that have produced those circumstances, and of what kinds of action might change them. Such understanding is somewhat akin to the fish of the Zen fable mentioned in chapter one actually *seeing* the sea it is immersed in for the first time, actually *noticing* for the first time that the sea is influenced by its many inhabitants and their needs as well as by natural forces, like tide and light. Paulo Freire has called this state, this acute awareness of the dynamics of one's environment, conscientization (1970). It provides a new goal for educators, and it is the subject of the next chapter.

Chapter Seven

REFOCUSING
Critical Consciousness/Conscientization

That weekend . . . was my awakening. I realized I didn't know who I was. I didn't have an Indian name. I didn't speak the Indian language. I didn't know the Indian customs. Dimly I remembered the Ottawa word for dog, but it was a baby word, *kahgee*, not the full word, *muhkahgee*, which I was later to learn. Even more hazily I remembered a naming ceremony (my own). I remembered legs dancing around me, dust. Where had that been? Who had I been?

Lewis P. Johnson

I remember a time when both of my children were very young and I discovered a watercolor scrawl on the blanket covering my daughter's bed. When I demanded of her *who* was responsible for the laundry dilemma now facing me, she immediately blamed her younger brother. Given that he had repeatedly demonstrated his boundless resourcefulness in creative destruction, and given that my daughter looked cherubic and nearly always acted so in public, I turned around and marched angrily toward my son's bedroom door. I was halfway down the hall before I realized that the scrawl spelled out my daughter's name—and that my son didn't yet know how to print.

Many parents, and nearly everyone else as well, have made such mistakes. By acting on *assumed* truths, we select a course of action that turns out to be mistaken when we pause to think more deeply. As discussed in chapter one, we confuse assumptions with the way things *are*, and our assumptions then provide a faulty foundation for our actions. I moved to punish my son, for example, because I assumed that one of my children could be counted on to tell the truth, and I assumed the other would be the culprit in any transgression. While this is a simplistic example, it demonstrates an important point to keep always in mind: what we *think* we know is not always a reliable guide for our actions, because much of what we think we know eventually proves untrue.

For example, many people learn as children that good men and women get married and live happily ever after; unlearning that lesson as their parents divorce is a devastating experience for many young people. Many children are also taught that all policemen are their friends, another lesson that often needs to be unlearned. My husband, for example, abandoned that idea when police roughed him up while taking him in for questioning about a crime he had nothing to do with; he was guilty only of being a young man in the wrong place at the wrong time. And, as a teenager I learned a similar lesson about authority when another driver ran a red light and totaled my car. When my insurance company called the police to obtain witnesses' names and numbers, we found that the police report had been falsified—and that the reckless driver was a police sergeant's son. No, some policemen are *not* our friends. Such contradictory lessons are not only painful, but powerful as well.

When some experience causes us to question our firmest beliefs about the world, there is a domino-like effect which can change our entire perspective both on who and where we are. When someone we trust lies to us, for example, we're likely to ask ourselves "If *that* person would lie to me, then who else can't I trust? How faulty is my judgment about people in general? Should I be less trusting? Should I do something to make clear to important people in my life that I must be able to believe them?" Similarly, the child whose parents are divorcing may ask, "If my parents won't keep our home together for my sake, can they love me? Can love *ever* last forever and ever? Should I continue to assume that I myself will someday be happily married? Should I be nice to members of the opposite sex, or just do as I please because no relationship is ever permanent anyway?" The youth treated harshly by police might ask "If the people who are supposed to protect me may harm me when I've done nothing wrong, how safe am I? What authority can I trust? Any? How do I know which ones, and when?"

Such chains of questioning, such probing of our assumptions, are elementary examples of a process Paulo Freire calls conscientization.

Critical theorists often name the state of mind that is nurtured by this process "critical consciousness." Critical consciousness is the mental habit of asking ourselves what assumptions are guiding our actions; why we believe what we believe; who gains and who loses from the assumptions we endorse; whether things might be otherwise, and possibly better; and how we might effect change if we think it desirable. Simply put, critical consciousness means that we adopt the habit of *not* taking the world for granted. Perhaps the process is best distilled in a gesture by the well-known critical educator Maxine Greene, who at one time gave all of her students bumper stickers bearing the challenge "Have You Questioned Anything Today?" (Mine is posted prominently on the bulletin board I face as I write.)

Critical theorists would argue that critical consciousness is not only a habit that all educators should cultivate, but also a goal that all educational efforts should serve.

AN AWAKENING TO POSSIBILITY

I have long been aware of the great debt I owe to one of my undergraduate professors, who triggered the beginning of my own critical consciousness with a casual remark she made in class. A brilliant woman and dramatic educator, she struck a pose in front of a literature class one day, stared off into a delightful, distant future only she could visualize, and made some exhortation beginning, "Now, when you go to Italy, you must . . . ." I've forgotten all the rest, but five of her words changed my future: "*when* you go to Italy." Not if. *When.*

In this class composed primarily of first-generation college students, mostly homebodies like me, the general reaction was an undercurrent of snickering. *As if* we were the kind of people who traveled abroad. *As if* we were the kind of people who would ever have enough money for such an extravagance. *As if* we were the kind of people who would ever develop the sophistication to master currency exchange, or even train schedules and subway maps. None of us traveled or thought about traveling abroad for the simple reason that we just didn't see ourselves as the kind of people who did that kind of thing.

And yet, this brilliant woman, who knew us well, had said *when*. And because *she* assumed someday I *would* go to Italy, I started thinking about my automatic assumption that I would *never* go. And so, of course, a few years later, I found a way to go. And I thought of her as I walked the streets of Rome, knowing that I would never have taken that trip without her remark, because without her remark it would never have *occurred* to me to want to go. But I did, and I learned a great deal—and not just about art and food.

I learned that even though I had grown up in a class of people who did not have the resources to travel abroad, I could find ways to sacrifice and save and pay for a trip I really wanted. I learned that even though I was a woman, I was capable of holding my own against would-be thieves and Romeos when in strange territory. I learned that, of course, there was no reason I couldn't learn to mentally translate thousands of lire into American dollars, and to read train and subway maps and schedules. (I'd learned plenty of other things, hadn't I? Why did I ever imagine I could *not* learn these?) Most importantly, I learned that what had been keeping me from traveling abroad was my own lack of imagination. I had absorbed certain assumptions from the culture around me about what kind of person I was, and about what that kind of person did or didn't do. I just never imagined I could do things differently than everyone around me.

Over the years, I've uncovered other assumptions that have confined me in ways I didn't have to accept, once I started thinking about and questioning my own ideas and actions. I learned, for example, that "good" wives don't have to do everything their husbands say. "Good" mothers aren't necessarily home or on duty twenty-four hours a day, seven days a week. Women can be good mothers and wives and human beings and still have an active mental and social life of their own. Men in authority aren't always right, just because they're men and have authority. I am perfectly capable of deciding what I want in a car and going out and purchasing it (something many women still can't imagine doing), and I no longer trust that clergy have a hotline to God. Among the hardest assumptions I ever managed to challenge, in fact, was the assumption that, having been born to the Catholic faith, I just *was* a Catholic forever and ever, amen. Now, my heart and soul tell me otherwise—but learning to listen to myself in this area was a long, painful, and yet ultimately liberating process.

Conscientization, while it sometimes involves blinding moments of clarity, is not something that happens one time, overnight. Instead, it is an ongoing process in which there is always something to learn about oneself and one's relation to the world. Having learned many lessons about how I mindlessly accepted assumptions about gender and class that limited my own possibilities, I was rudely jarred by another kind of lesson recently. Leading a book group in which texts were chosen by a funding agency, I was exposed to Nadine Gordimer's novel *July's People*. I found that book profoundly disturbing and am still working on figuring out what it means to me in terms of my own choices. Simply put, the novel forced me to this confrontation with myself: "OK, Hinchey, you've come a long way in figuring out who oppresses you and how, and how you limit your own horizons. Now, whose horizons do *you* limit? Whom do *you* oppress? Who pays for the privileges *you* enjoy?"

All of us exist at some station in the world, better off than some, worse off than others. Any privilege we enjoy is likely to have come from someone else's sacrifice. As a tenure-track university faculty member, I set my own teaching schedule; who is inconvenienced by that, and what needs do they subsequently have trouble meeting? Does an exploited mother who teaches part-time have difficulty arranging child care just so that I can have the selfish schedule of my dreams? I can buy fresh strawberries any time of year, and amazingly cheaply at times. Who picks them, and how little pay must they accept to allow me to buy fruit as cheaply as I do? What has the commercial farming of large tracts of land, the kind of farming that stocks supermarkets serving spoiled families like mine, cost small farmers and residents of areas where agricultural chemicals affect land and air quality? How do I justify paying the rent on a Cape Cod cabin for lazy weeks in the summer, when children in nearby Boston lack medical care, dental care, and even food?

Disturbing questions, whose answers I've yet to find. And this is precisely why the idea of critical teaching is so threatening to so many people. Once the challenging of assumptions begins, the train of thought often leads farther and farther into the most taken-for-granted elements of our lives, a terribly threatening and unsettling process for anyone with any privilege at all. We all like to think of ourselves as fair and just; believing that we've *earned* the privilege we have does a great deal to allow us to enjoy our privilege in good conscience. But what if we *haven't* earned what we've got, what if the color of our skin or our gender has unfairly affected our fate? And/or, what if others pay a high price for our privilege, with their health, welfare, and comfort?

From the perspective of the critical theorist, however, the fact that the process is difficult and unsettling does not change the fact that it's necessary. If we are to make education *truly* empowering, if we are to *really* equip students to live their lives actively and honestly, then students *must* learn to question their unconscious assumptions and to uncover choices they have no idea are open to them. My revelation about my ability to travel offers a mild demonstration of how powerfully assumptions shape our actions. But closer to the classroom, my experience with my undergraduate education students offers a frightening demonstration of how teachers' assumptions can shape their own actions and so their students' futures.

CRITICAL CONSCIOUSNESS AND TOMORROW'S TEACHERS

When I first thought through how I might present the idea of critical consciousness to undergraduates in my theory class, I decided that a short story by Toni Cade Bambara, "The Lesson," would be a perfect introduction.[1] I felt sure that the story would make them see immediately what I was talking about. Instead, my assumption about the effect of the story proved faulty, and I got a memorable lesson in how beliefs that my students mistake for truth confine their understanding and vision.

In this story, Miss Moore, an educated African-American woman from Harlem, takes a group of neighborhood children downtown to the upscale toy store, F.A.O. Schwarz, on elegant Fifth Avenue in New York City. The children, whose families have limited financial resources, have never been to such an extravagant store and find it intimidating. Sylvia, the young narrator, reports that when they arrive

> I kinda hang back. Not that I'm scared, what's there to be afraid of . . . . But I feel funny, shame. But what I got to be shamed about? Got as much right to go in as anybody. But somehow I can't seem to get hold of the door. (615)

The children sense that this is a place not intended for them even before they enter. Once inside, they are stunned by the price of the toys, exclaiming over a $480 paperweight, admiring a $1,000 sailboat, and discussing the boats they themselves make for a single dollar.

Stationed at the back of a subway train on the return to Harlem, Sylvia ponders what she has seen, demonstrating the kind of questioning central to critical consciousness. Instead of simply pitying herself for not being able to shop at the store, she starts wondering who *does* shop there, how they attained their privileged position, and how she herself came to be in a far less privileged slot:

> I'm thinkin about this tricky toy I saw in the store. A clown that somersaults on a bar then does chin-ups just cause you yank lightly at his leg. Cost $35. I could see me askin my mother for a $35 birthday clown. "You wanna who that costs what?" she'd say, cocking her head to the side to get a better view of the hole in my head. Thirty-five dollars could buy new bunk beds for Junior and Gretchen's boy. Thirty-five dollars and the whole household could go visit Grandaddy Nelson in the country. Thirty-five dollars would pay for the rent and the piano bill too. Who are these people that spend that much for performing clowns and $1000 for toy sailboats? What kinda work they do and how they live and how come we ain't in on it? Where we are is who we are, Miss Moore always pointin out. But it don't necessarily have to be that way, she always adds then waits for somebody to say that poor people have to wake up and demand their share of the pie and don't none of us know what kind of pie she talking about in the first damn place. (615)

Back in Harlem discussing the day, Sylvia's friend Sugar notes that she doesn't think "all of us here put together eat in a year what that sailboat costs" and goes on to conclude that "this is not much of a democracy if you ask me. Equal chance to pursue happiness means an equal crack at the dough, don't it?" Sylvia, who seems to have had similar thoughts, goes off by herself at the story's end "to think this day through," insisting in the last line that "ain't nobody gonna beat me at nuthin." The trip downtown into alien territory has caused her to question boundaries in her life that she had earlier accepted without question.

I had hoped that my students would see in the story an example of how the less privileged might start to develop more insight about where they are in relation to others, about how vast the discrepancies in wealth are between classes. As Sylvia notes, the poor keep hearing that they have to "wake up and demand their share of the pie" when they have no idea what pie there is to be shared in the first place. Prior to this trip, the children had never been in a wealthy area and had no idea what exactly it meant in practical terms when they heard their neighborhood referred to as "the ghetto." They could not imagine $1,000 toys before they saw them, as I could not imagine traveling abroad until someone else told me I could.

Unlike Sylvia and her friend, however, my own students did not grasp the idea that the social conditions reflected in the story are *conditions*, not some fixed reality, not the way the world *has* to be. In fact, they unconsciously assume that things *are* the way they *have* to be, the only way they *can* be. Because they confuse beliefs with facts, they fail to understand Sylvia's questioning. Here, for example, are some typical responses from reaction papers my students wrote immediately after I read the story to them.

> The whole money situation seems so unfair and in some cases it is. It may not be fair, but it is how our society was supposed to work, how the founding fathers wanted it to work.

> Money shouldn't be the way you judge people, but it is. I used to babysit for a woman's grandchildren who would order things from Macy's and Tiffany's. I always felt a little intimidated by it but now I know it's okay to have nice things if you can afford them. But that's okay because I know it's Tiffany's and Macy's for them, but it's Sears and J.C. Penney's for me.

My students are resigned to huge inequities not only for others, but for themselves, because they see the situation as beyond control, just some inherited and fixed fact.

There is a particular irony here in that my students' responses reflect the same sorts of lack of privilege as the children in the story, albeit on a slightly more privileged level. The children in the story make their toys from cheap supplies; my students get theirs from Sears and Penney's. The privileged shop at F.A.O. Schwarz; generally, my students say they've never been to that exclusive store, nor could they afford to shop there because of the same restrictions the Harlem children face.

Moreover, my students are familiar with Sylvia's sense of not belonging, of somehow being ashamed when in the territory of the very rich:

I can understand how they felt when they went into the store because when I go into rich stores—like a few times I went to the Ryah House—whenever I go into places like that I feel out of place.

The children from the poor part of town feel ashamed to be around those from the rich part of town. I can see why they are like that. I don't live in the poor part of town, nor the rich, but I feel awkward around people from the "rich section" of my town.

When [the characters] went into that store and a feeling of inferiority came over them, it made me remember my vacation in Florida. One day we ate breakfast in the Grand Floridian Hotel, one of the premier resorts, and when I walked in I felt a little inferior.

Like the characters in the story, my students know that some places are not meant for them, that they should not expect to have the means to go where some go. But they are so immersed in their culture and its unchallenged assumptions that they fail to question how and why current conditions exist—even when the children in the story do. They know their place, and they accept it. Moreover, they accept current conditions as fixed even as they express faith in the idea that America offers equal opportunity to everyone.

[Miss Moore] knew that if she didn't teach the kids about social and economic lifestyles they would be doomed to repeat their parents' lifestyle. . . . She made them see that with determination and striving they too someday can afford expensive things. It's up to the individual to determine what kind of life they want to have. She was letting the children know that they have a choice.

Apparently, my students don't stop to wonder why, if all people really do have a choice, everyone doesn't choose luxury. Several students, not seeing this glitch in reasoning, similarly express the conviction that if only all poor children "set their goals high, then they too [can] afford such things one day."

Perhaps they are able to explain away the puzzle of why the poor would *choose* to be poor because they also frequently accept another cultural maxim accepted as self-evident truth: "Blessed are the poor."

> It really doesn't matter if you have a $30,000 car and a huge extravagant house. As long as you are healthy and loved, those other things shouldn't matter at all.

> I like to think that it is not how much we have, but how much we enjoy that makes happiness.

> Most people think about poor people as less fortunate and are sad for them. But it doesn't seem that anyone is sad for rich people or think that they are less fortunate, when in some cases they are less fortunate because of their ignorance and selfishness. It seems these things are not found as frequently in poor people. They seem to be more willing to share and help others with what they can.

For students who themselves don't believe they'll ever be shopping at F. A. O. Schwarz, it seems more useful to endorse philanthropy and to ponder the supposed benefits of *not* being wealthy than it does to question why wealth is distributed so inequitably. In just this way is perpetuated, when the people who have least endorse such cultural maxims as "Bloom where you're planted," or "Make the best of a bad situation," or "Money isn't everything."

I know I've been discussing my students' reactions at length, but I think there's good reason to focus on this group. The literature tells us that education students come from primarily white, middle-class backgrounds, and this is certainly true of my students. I believe that in many ways they are typical of education students nationwide—and I think that if their thinking, as it reveals itself in these comments, is indeed representative, then it has terrifying implications for schools and children.

Specifically, if tomorrow's teachers cannot imagine our society structured differently than it currently is, if they cannot imagine prosperity even for themselves, then how are they to work effectively to provide *their* students with the imagination necessary to attempt a better future? I went to Italy because a teacher told me I could; students with limited horizons *must* have teachers who routinely introduce them to new possibilities. How will teachers who lack imagination in their *own* lives pry open the imagination of their students?

No one ever changed anything by looking at a situation and simply saying "Well, it's too bad that's the way it is, but that *is* the way it is, and it's not going to change no matter what I do." In fact, a world of immorality (slavery, rape, vigilante hangings) existed tenaciously because too many people shrugged atrocities off with this attitude. If people who don't go to bed hungry accept as inevitable the fact that some people do, how can they contribute to an educational system that is *supposed* to empower children to free themselves from such conditions?

Time and again, my students react in ways that deny the possibility that things can be other than they are. When I show them the videotape discussed at length above, for example, they routinely insist that Lonnie (like the children in the story) can "make it" if he "just works hard enough." The question of *how* Lonnie will magically become equipped to compete with James and his classmates on the kinds of tests used for sorting in New York City's competitive high schools remains, for my students, an irrelevant abstraction. Working with cases asking them to imagine themselves in specific teaching situations, my students consistently reveal how deeply they accept the idea that things *can't* change.

One case, for example, creates a situation in which a poor student and a rich student commit the same offense but are given very different punishments. Asked to choose between defending the poor student (and risking administrative wrath) and keeping silent (and not rocking the boat), my students overwhelmingly fail to see any choice at all. "Well, you *can't* do anything that might get you fired," they insist. "It would be dumb to risk your paycheck." In another case, where they must choose between accepting merit pay (and endorsing a demonstrably unfair and unsound merit pay system) or refusing it (risking administrative anger and forfeiting the cash), again they choose overwhelmingly to take the money and protect their own interests, seeing the "choice" as self-evident. All too well they have learned the competitive lesson of American capitalism: "Every man for himself." Ethics, justice, loyalty, and the larger good be damned; they never even enter the picture my students visualize.

From time to time, I ask a class this question: "Do you think it's possible that a prerequisite to being a *really* good teacher is a willingness to get fired for something really important?" And they respond, routinely: "*WHAT?*"

Only two in a marriage, and they must be heterosexual. A person must always place his or her own income and privilege above any other consideration. That's just the way it is.

CRITICAL CONSCIOUSNESS AND TODAY'S TEACHERS

Obviously, much of the thinking detailed in the section above is also shown by teachers currently in classrooms. In fact, many recurring teachers' lounge comments indicate that such thinking probably *is* common among teachers: "I don't bother about trying that with *these* kids." "Where *these* kids are headed, they're not going to have to know much anyway." "I taught the father, and now I've got the son, and you know, the apple never falls far from the tree." A sense of fatalism, particularly about children from disadvantaged homes, pervades schools, even as we hail them as oases of equal opportunity. Until this thinking changes, little else is likely to change.

But even teachers who *do* genuinely believe in the ability and potential of their students, who *can* imagine a fate for children different than their parents', may hold other, rarely questioned assumptions that prevent them from pursuing change. Any number of current beliefs about schooling impede teachers' ability to conceive, let alone undertake, productive efforts to change the way things currently are.

Perhaps the hardest mindset to question is that associated with positivism. When I was younger, I was so deeply ingrained in Catholicism that I wasn't even *aware* of being Catholic, despite Sunday masses and weekly catechism. Similarly, so many teachers were themselves nurtured in positivism that they aren't even aware that they act on positivist precepts. As already noted in chapter one, *the* prevalent model of teaching is of "teacher as expert," transmitting expert information. Schooling is about students acquiring heaps of facts, figures, dates, and data.

When teachers do anything other than lecture or assign standardized seat work, they suffer nagging guilt, suggesting that if they aren't talking, or if all students are silently working at their seats, then learning isn't happening and they aren't doing their jobs. (As it never occurred to me to ask myself why I should be able to handle a course in statistics but not a foreign train schedule, it rarely occurs to teachers to ask why they assume learning *is* happening just because they're talking and students are reasonably quiet.) Or, since student-centered, collaborative learning often results in students making mistakes and rarely results in neat, standard results, teachers feel that with alternative approaches students may not get enough course content fast enough. Positivism permeates their subconscious, sending them back time and again to force-feeding information into students, who are made to depend entirely on the teacher.

For this to change, teachers have to start asking themselves hard questions about what school is *for*. If they agree that the purpose of school is to transmit information, then they can go right on lecturing. But if they think that instead of *having* information students ought to be able to find things out independently, to make sense of data on their own, then they need to realize that there is no sense in feeling guilty about not having "taught" Chapter 20. Stuffing kids with facts is one thing, helping them develop their own skills so that they can function independently, as lifelong learners, is quite another.

At this point in any discussion with teachers, I normally encounter the "Yeah, but" reaction, another indication of positivism at work.

Yeah, you're right, but my principal won't let me do that.

Yeah, you're right, but the curriculum guide says I HAVE to cover everything up to Chapter 22.

Yeah, you're right, but my kids have to take standardized tests, and they have to be ready.

Here is precisely the same form of fatalism my undergraduates exhibit when they say that a teacher can't refuse merit pay, or can't stand up for a student treated unfairly, because that's the way things *are* and it's impossible to change them. But there's an enormous difference between being *unable* to do something and being *unwilling* to do it because it's difficult.

My students are wrong about not having a choice. They *could* make choices involving self-sacrifice. And teachers are wrong. Change *is* possible. Perhaps the principal can be persuaded to allow change. Perhaps he or she can be persuaded by parents whom the teacher enlisted to support a new idea. Or perhaps by a deluge of research articles supporting the proposal. Or by being taken to visit a school where the strategy is working. And if the curriculum guide says that Chapter 22 must be covered, does it say *how*? Why can't students read it and be responsible for it on their own? Why can't teachers type, copy, and distribute information they feel students *must* have instead of lecturing? Why can't the main points of Chapter 20 be covered in a thematic approach, combined logically with main points of Chapters 4, 12, and 18? Or be the base of independent research projects? And why can't the curriculum guide itself be changed?

Working with inservice teachers has taught me that they are limited by lack of imagination more than anything else. This is *not* meant as a critical statement, but as a description of the logical result of a very faulty educational process. Students in schools, including colleges of education, learn what they are taught. In recent history, teacher educators have done a bang-up job of teaching teachers to be passive, conforming, authoritative, inflexible, unimaginative, apolitical, and silent. Any imagination that reared its head during their education courses was likely to be directed toward designing attractive bulletin boards, rather than toward designing exciting learning opportunities for children or influencing policy in schools.

Positivism has led to teachers relying on texts to guide the teaching and to inflexible teaching strategies that specify fixed amounts of time (in bits or seconds) for doing this or that; disciplinary "systems" fix graduated penalties for the "crime" of talking sociably to one's peers in a classroom and other infractions, eliminating any need for the teacher to think about student behavior. (Am I the only one who wonders how many graduate students would be sent to the academic dean for talking in class if professors used the sort of strategies they preach to others? Or how many education professors would forfeit their raises if someone quizzed them and found out they were incapable of specifying a class objective in behavioral terms?)

Because teachers often receive these "rules" from "expert" professors in positivist college classrooms, they assume that any ideas their own experience offers are inferior to this received wisdom. And so, when they stray from the norm, doing good things in classrooms by instinct and compassion, they also routinely "apologize" for their hereticism when talking about such episodes. I cannot count the number of times I've heard a teacher say "I know I probably shouldn't be doing this, but in my classroom sometimes I . . . ." Invariably what follows this disclaimer is description of a *constructivist* practice that experience has proven useful.

All of this circles around the issue of authority, where again received wisdom inhibits teachers' imaginations. If the positivist world that teachers have experienced is credible (and they begin by having to assume it is, as I had to begin by assuming the rightness of Catholicism—there was nowhere else I could see to go), then the hierarchies that are in place make sense. Education professors must know best about what constitutes good classroom practice; principals must know best about good policies for schools; the experts who write textbooks must know best about how to divide and sequence subject matter; teachers must certainly have complete authority *over* children (as others in the hierarchy have authority over them) by virtue of their advanced age, experience, and knowledge.

And, as the authoritative teachers remain committed to an agenda set by "experts" and removed from students' lives, they negate the identities and experiences students bring with them from worlds of different backgrounds. By trying to shove students into a fixed mold, they generate more and more and more resistance among students who don't match the cultural template, causing more and more criticism of schools and more and more antagonism on the part of teachers themselves. Even when they recognize the negative effects of what they do, however, teachers feel that they have neither any right nor any power to change it.

Believing that they themselves have authority only over students, teachers don't challenge the authorities who make lousy choices and set lousy policies. Grumble in the lounge? Yes. Challenge openly, thoughtfully, collaboratively, productively? No. But again, why should they, if they believe that the world they inhabit cannot be changed, that it's fixed somewhere, somehow, by authorities who have earned their powerful positions by virtue of having worked harder or by simply being smarter?

And so the hegemony of the privileged continues without challenge, and what is actually a tissue of assumption about the way things *are* becomes a self-fulfilling prophecy: the world *doesn't* change.

But if you're a critical theorist that doesn't stop you from remembering that it *can*.

PEDAGOGY FOR CRITICAL CONSCIOUSNESS

The fact that we can't make choices until we recognize choices has profound implications. Uncovering our choices, as discussed earlier in this chapter, involves the process of questioning our most taken-for-granted ideas. To become change agents in the world, students need to learn how to question their daily experience. To effectively mentor students through this learning process, teachers themselves must develop the habit of subjecting their own habits and assumptions to the same sort of questioning.

Freire believes that all education, all critical questioning, ought to be grounded in daily experience so that students can come to recognize what they've accepted by default because they are blinded by assumption. What are our mental and physical habits? Where did they come from? Who gains what, who loses what, because of our habits? How might things be otherwise? If teachers focus such questions on familiar events of daily life, then even young children can be introduced to a critical approach to the world.

For example, children in elementary school might be asked to talk about what cereal they commonly eat for breakfast. Why do they or their caregivers select that particular cereal? Is it good for them? How would they know? If it's not nutritious, and they know that, why do they eat it anyway, to their body's disadvantage? What role, for example, might television advertising or peer opinion have played in their selection? Are their eating habits typical in households in their community? If so, and if they think other habits may be better, how might they go about trying to change the community's behavior?

The process works much the same way with teachers. Generally, most teachers give tests. Why? What exactly makes it *necessary* to give the same test to every student in the class? Who benefits from this practice? How? Who loses? How? What factors besides student knowledge might affect test results? What do those factors indicate about the reliability of the test? How else might teachers assess students' progress? Who would gain what, who would lose what, with various forms of alternative assessment?

As I thought about an example to develop this point about common practices, I was sorely tempted to explore the topic of spelling in elementary schools. Ultimately, I chose not to, because I've had too many elementary school teachers stare at me as if I were crazy while they exhaled an incredulous "*WHAT?*" in response to my question "Why do you teach and grade spelling as a separate subject?" The assumption that there must be a subject called spelling in elementary schools and that it must be graded separately is so ingrained that it may be virtually impossible for many teachers to challenge it early on in the process of their conscientization. For readers willing to tackle the nearly inconceivable, however, I'd suggest thinking hard about this subject. Why is spelling a sacred entity in elementary schools? Why are spelling textbooks used and spelling tests given? Why x-number of words per week, no more, no fewer? Who gains what, who loses what, in this system? And so on.

Until teachers can find new ways to explore what has previously seemed unthinkable, little will change in schools. If the poet Robert Frost hadn't seen two paths in front of him, we never would have had his famous poem about his choice to take the road less traveled. Whether the neglected road existed or not, if he hadn't noticed it, for all practical purposes he would have had no choice to make.

YEAH, BUT . . .

. . . what happens when we raise all this consciousness? What happens when we start seeing choices where before there were none? What exactly do critical theorists think teachers ought to be doing in classrooms? And what would *curriculum* look like? Surely no one thinks we should have kids sit around all day talking about cereals, even if they might learn some things about nutrition along the way. What does all this theory *mean* in terms of individual teachers working with kids in classrooms?

Without praxis, it means nothing. And so, chapter seven attends to that critical topic.

Note

1. Parts of this chapter were previously published in the spring 1997 issue of *Teaching Education.*

Chapter Eight

SO AFTER THEORY, WHAT?
Praxis and Empowerment

We alone can devalue gold
by not caring
if it falls or rises
in the marketplace.
Alice Walker

The reason that many teachers are reluctant to discuss theory is that, to their minds, it never "goes" anywhere in relation to the classroom. "Well, that's interesting," they may think, "but what does it mean in terms of what I'm supposed to do in my classroom on Monday morning? What's supposed to *happen* if I buy into this?" This chapter will offer a variety of suggestions in answer to that question, so that interested readers have a menu of practical starting points to choose from when they close this book. Experience tells me, however, that until I answer some common challenges to critical theory, some readers will be reluctant to go any further down this theoretical road. Therefore, before considering classroom implications (summarized in the concepts of empowerment and praxis), I'll try to clear some common objections out of the way.

CRITICISMS OF THE THEORY

Critical theory is not realistic. To be honest, when I've talked seriously about critical theory to colleagues, one of the most common reactions I've encountered has been sniggering: "Those are sweet ideas, Pollyanna. You just keep working on them, keeping an eye out for some Spanish guy who's out there with you charging at windmills." Modern American culture is highly idealistic on the surface, but it currently has a thoroughly cynical streak at its core.

"This is a competitive society," many say, "as it has to be if it's to be a successfully capitalist one. Every man [and, some add grudgingly, woman] has no choice but to look out for Number One. You're talking about trying to even things out; who is going to buy into that? Robin Hood has been dead a long time, and people who now have power aren't going to be interested in his resurrection." Dreaming the impossible dream makes great lyrics for Broadway musicals, but it's a lousy approach to everyday life, they say.

Critics frequently charge, in short, that the theory is utopian. Well, OK, so it is. Freire himself uses the word *utopian* to describe the work of critical educators. And what's wrong with that?

However cynical many Americans have become, critical theorists argue that it is still reasonable to work toward a more just, ethical, and moral world. After all, what are our alternatives? Consider the impact of prevalent, rarely questioned ideas in today's American society. Peter McLaren aptly summarizes the prevailing cultural mindset as one that has created a world where we've

> normalized greed, the right to be racist, the logic of self-interest, a desire for private gain, and a hatred for conscientious dissent . . . where hope is held hostage, where justice is lashed to the altar of capital accumulation, and where the good works of our collective citizenry have been effaced by despair. (21)

This may be the way things are now, but critical theorists reject that this is the way they *have* to be.

"But how far do you think you're going to get trying to change things?" ask some. "Given that humankind has always exhibited greedy and violent behavior, isn't the critical theorists' pursuit of a just world an impossible dream? Aren't you kidding yourselves to think these conditions are going to change significantly?" Maybe. Maybe not. But I believe there are two points that make worrying about exactly how much of our dream we can accomplish irrelevant. First, what is the alternative to working for change? And second, isn't acting justly as individual human beings more important than how close we come to our goal?

No matter what we do, as chapter one suggested, our actions support *someone's* agenda. If we simply accept the world as it is, as being fixed, shrugging off its imperfections as inevitable, we *contribute* to the perpetuation of the way things are. We allow the hegemony of current assumptions to go unchallenged, in effect supporting the current fraudulent system. Those who find this alternative unacceptable don't *have* to passively accept it. They can choose instead to work for change. And working for change requires that we reconceptualize education, so that it becomes a genuine source of opportunity rather than a means of perpetuating the status quo. Formulating a vision of education that makes it a tool for change means, in McLaren's words,

> that educators must begin candidly and critically to face our society's complicity in the roots and structures of inequality and injustice. It means, too, that as teachers we must face our own culpability in the reproduction of inequality in our teaching, and that we must strive to develop a pedagogy equipped to provide both intellectual and moral resistance to oppression, one that extends the concept of pedagogy beyond the mere transmission of knowledge and skills and the concept of morality beyond interpersonal relations. (21)

Yes, critical theorists are idealistic. But given the alternative—cynicism and passive support for the unjust way things *are*—I would argue that their idealism is a strength rather than a weakness. Their vision can help move us in the direction of a better world.

"But what is the *point* of turning in that direction when the goal is unrealistic? Just look at history, and you *know* you are not going to be able to cultivate a just world." As is often the case with philosophical questions, literature offers some appropriate food for thought. For example, a character named Hattie in Barbara Kingsolver's novel *Animal Dreams* sees the oppression in government policy so clearly that she leaves home to help field-workers in Nicaragua grow food. When her sister Codi starts thinking of her as some kind of saint because she's devoting her life to what seems an impossible dream, and starts treating Hattie with nearly religious awe, the idealist becomes angry and puts her efforts in sharp perspective for skeptics. From Hattie's perspective, it's not whether or not she can reach the goal that matters; what's important is how she lives her life.

> It's not some perfect ideal we're working toward that keeps us going. . . . I don't expect
> to see perfection before I die. . . . What keeps you going isn't some fine destination but
> just the road you're on, and the fact that you know how to drive. (224)

Or, as the poet Robert Browning put it, "A man's reach must exceed his grasp, or what's a heaven for?" Or Camus: "The struggle itself toward the heights is enough to fill one's heart." Isn't living a moral life, acting on behalf of justice, reason enough to join in the struggle? Shouldn't teachers, of all people, take "the other" into account when we chart the course of our professional lives? Doesn't being a professional require ethical responsibility and demand that we lobby on behalf of the best interests of our students?

Educators do normally think of themselves as working on behalf of children, and most of them sincerely want to help ensure all children a bright future. The fact that no one teacher can change reality for every student has *never* prevented people from entering the profession. Why should teachers reject working toward the critical theorists' utopian dream of a just world when they have already accepted the discouraging truth that every teacher faces: they will never succeed with every student entrusted to their care. If they accept partial success as a limit to what they already do on a daily basis, why not accept partial success in pursuit of an equitable world? This is especially true in the face of the specific goals of critical theory, which are at the same time impossibly grand and strikingly basic. Hattie outlines them in their starkest simplicity:

> What I want is so simple I almost can't say it: elementary kindness. Enough to eat,
> enough to go around. The possibility that kids might one day grow up to be neither the
> destroyers nor the destroyed. (299)

No racism, sexism, lookism, classism, or any other *ism*. Minimally, decent living conditions for every human being. True democracy, rather than rhetorical democracy. Isn't any step closer to these goals worth the struggle? Doesn't attempting these goals make any person's life richer, more purposeful, more ethical, more worth living?

Critical theory is political. Pursuing the goal of genuine democracy means that education must become a means of enabling people to make changes in their social reality. They need to understand how power works and how they might go about challenging the current structure, taking more power into their own hands. But of course, equipping people to challenge the status quo is a blatantly political goal. And that realization yields another common criticism of critical theory and pedagogy: "You're making education political. You ought to allow schools to be places for teaching and to leave politics out of it."

The problem is, however, that there *is* no way to "leave politics out of it." Schooling is *inevitably* political, politics are *always* involved; the only question is whether we are to be open about that or not. For example, the question of what to teach is a political question. Do we choose to include the history of women and Native Americans in textbooks or not? And if so, to what extent? Anyone who doubts that these are significant political questions should read news accounts of the bloody battles over the first draft of national standards for social studies. To hear some conservatives tell the story, the folks doing the drafting were infidels plotting to overthrow our philanthropic, God-fearing government. On the other side, defenders were arguing that traditional textbooks were designed to keep a white, male, European-American model as the cultural template for what an "American" (or at least, an American who *matters*) looks, sounds, and acts like. With national political figures vocally taking sides, who can doubt the political nature of curriculum?

Countless other practices lived out daily in classrooms have equally political (if less obvious) implications, however neutral they may seem on the surface. For example, does the teacher take the role of expert authority with all the right answers, discouraging students from trying to design their own answers to questions and from asking provocative questions? Or, does the teacher take the role of the most experienced learner in a community of learners, encouraging student questioning and independent thinking? Choosing between these roles is a political act because each will affect how students ultimately perceive their role in relation to authority. By example, authoritative practices imply that students have no business questioning expert authority, while collaborative practices suggest that students have both the right and the ability to ask questions and formulate their own answers.

Either decision has important implications for the kinds of citizens students will eventually become. Those who were taught not to challenge authority, who accepted the expert teacher's word as law, are likely to passively accept the word of government experts on such topics as whether it's time to have a war or whether we ought to spend billions on a space project. Those who were taught that they have the right and the ability to question everything are likely to feel, in contrast, that there's no need to accept the word of any expert as unbiased and necessarily the best one. They know how to find information on topics they care about, and they know how to weigh evidence on both sides and reach their own conclusions. Of course, this sort of person is much less docile when people in power try to lead them this way or that. Which kind of citizen will seem more desirable to *whom*?

Again, what teachers do in classrooms will support *someone's* agenda, whether they are conscious of their support or not. Teachers can either go along with the widespread policies, like teaching standardized texts and giving one-right-answer tests, that make schools a mechanism for social reproduction—or they can take an oppositional stance, working on behalf of a kind of education that will allow the disadvantaged to compete more effectively for power. If they don't choose consciously, then they will act on behalf of the status quo by default, and the consequences of their actions will be the same as if they decided to champion the privileged.

Yes, critical theory is utopian and political. But neither of those adjectives deserves the negative connotations that critics have tried to assign them.

Critical theory engenders despair. When my students heard me read "The Lesson," the short story discussed in chapter six about the Harlem children who visit F.A.O. Schwarz, many of them were critical of Miss Moore for showing the children a world they can't expect to live in. Why, my students asked, expose kids to everything they *don't* have and make them unhappy? In such criticisms, my students echo many educators who worry that critical consciousness will lead only to unhappiness:

> I know from personal experience that the knowledge of high lifestyles sometimes depresses me—the thought that while I can barely afford my bills because of college expenses, there are people spending millions every day on the "finer things."

After hearing this story, I have doubts whether we should show the children a different world when we can't provide a way for them to escape from the old one. That could only lead to violence at the anger they feel for not being able to advance. I don't know if it's fair to them when we know the reality of the situation they are in.

I've heard teachers of children from blue-collar homes make much the same argument: "These kids aren't going anywhere but to McDonald's or the docks. Why not help them see that as a good thing instead of filling their heads with ideas that are going to lead them to be dissatisfied with their lives?" The suggestion here is that "Ignorance is bliss"—that what people don't know can't hurt them. Children can't pine for a $1,000 toy if they've never seen and can't imagine one. If wanting what we can't have will make us unhappy, then we're better off not knowing what others have, according to this perspective.

However, this is more hegemony at work, more unquestioning acceptance that the way things are is the way they must be. But, in reality, there is only one certainty in current conditions: things are unlikely to change significantly if the less privileged and powerful are kept blind to the kinds of lives others live. If they can't imagine the kind of privilege others enjoy, then they can't *pursue* similar privileges—a larger piece of the pie—for themselves. And *that* is an obvious advantage for those who currently have power. The student quoted above is right, actually, to worry about violence: coming to see that they've been treated unfairly without seeing any hope that things will improve *does* lead the disenfranchised to rage, and often violence as well. Americans are not strangers to riots in poor communities. Passion that cannot be channeled into a productive outlet cannot be indefinitely contained, and if violence becomes the only action people perceive possible, then they may well act violently. When there appears to be no other outlet for despair, people who come to understand how they've been cheated and deceived may choose acts of crime and violence. (Or, sadly, if they are incapable of either violence or passive acceptance, they may escape into the numbing substance abuse they are so often criticized for.)

It is precisely because critical consciousness could lead to despair and/or violence that an essential element of critical theory is praxis: *action* based on reflection. Critical consciousness is indispensable to envision change, but it is also insufficient to realize it. A critical educator is not someone who simply understands the tenets of critical theory; instead, a critical educator is someone who *acts* consciously in accordance with those tenets.

If critical questioning never leads to action, then the process is incomplete.

PRAXIS: WORKING FOR CHANGE

A grain of truth often appears even in criticism that we reject on the whole. Practitioners often criticize theory and theorists as being impractical, ephemeral, and useless; theorists criticize atheoretical practitioners as being bumbling at best, harmful at worst. The grain of truth within *both* charges is well understood by critical theorists: any time we divorce theory and practice, we run the risk of dangerous conditions eloquently summarized by critical educators Knoblach and Brannon:

> If theory unresponsive to practice is at best empty talk and at worst an academic power trip at the expense of other people, teaching without theoretical articulateness is a product of unthinking custom, accident, and the impositions of others, with no less potential (perhaps more, in fact) for taking advantage of the powerless. (9)

Neither situation is acceptable. If practitioners are to be consistent and effective, they must be guided by theory they endorse explicitly; they must consciously match their actions to goals they endorse, avoiding mindlessly supporting someone else's agenda. But if theory is to be useful as a guide to action, then its implications for real world action must be made clear by theorists.

In critical theory, the need for action is embodied in the concept of praxis, already defined above: action based on reflection. How might practitioners start translating critical theory to action? By first adopting a questioning attitude toward their own worlds, consciously examining and rethinking daily events and their own assumptions about the way things *have* to be. That is, the first step toward becoming a critical educator is to cultivate one's own critical consciousness. "How did things come to be as they are in my school, my neighborhood, my profession? Who benefits, at whose expense? Is this good? If not, what changes might make things better? And what exactly is my definition of better? Why?" But such questioning is only the beginning. When educators reach new understandings by thinking things through from new perspectives, then they must design their personal praxis. That is, they must identify actions they themselves will take to seek the changes they believe desirable. And, of course, they must actually execute the actions they've identified.

My own growth in feminism illustrates the process. Only in recent years have I thought consciously about how women are disadvantaged in American society, starting to question *why* so many men I know have power over others while many women have little power over even their own lives. And only very recently have I thought through my praxis in relation to sexism and gender equity. For years, I deferred automatically to men, like principals, in authoritative positions; I was acting with constructed consciousness, cooperating with my own subjugation by obediently following policies set by others without question, even if I thought they were harmful. Even a few short years ago, when a colleague and I were greeted and repeatedly referred to as "girls" by a principal, I said nothing. Oh, I fumed silently and complained to my colleague later—but I took no *productive* action to stop the behavior I found unacceptable, or to discourage the principal from doing it again, either to me or some other woman. I had made progress in critical consciousness, realizing that such diminutive terms help keep women in subordinate positions, and so I was offended and angry—but silent, and so I cooperated in allowing things to go on as before.

At that time, although my understanding of current conditions had increased, I hadn't yet defined my own sense of what I might *do* about them—and so I did nothing. And by keeping silent, I failed to act as a critical educator. I had no praxis. But today, having carefully thought through power and gender issues as I see them, I have an arsenal of strategies to change what I don't like about the treatment of women:

If anyone uses demeaning language to refer to women, I politely but firmly object.

If I see an image I find demeaning to women in the media, I explain to my children (or anyone else near me) why I find the image offensive.

I consciously mentor my female students, calling their passivity to their attention and modeling how they might be firm in resisting oppression without being oppressive themselves.

I work hard to persuade females who are victims of harassment to report incidents to appropriate authorities.

I watch administrative responses to incidents and provide feedback—both positive and negative—to responsible supervisors about how one feminist perceives their actions. (Of course, not all administrators welcome comments on their decisions, but I believe that as a member of the community I have a right and responsibility to tell those with power how well I think they're using it.)

I include gender equity as a topic in courses, and in my courses I also frequently criticize media portrayals of women (as I criticize rhetorical abuse of statistics).

I lobby for educational programs on the subject of sexism and sexual harassment.

I have been trained to offer gender equity workshops.

I read, a lot, about gender issues, including criticisms of feminists and feminist work.

No doubt I've left out many things, but this should make the point. Praxis involves figuring out what we can do to contribute to change—and then doing it.

Praxis is the mechanism of change: "If this is what I believe about how things are and how things *should* be, then what actions do I take to support the goals I endorse and inhibit the conditions I don't like?" It's not helpful to act without thinking (as I did during my early years of teaching, when I passively accepted the right of male authorities to control my classroom situation without input from me); it's equally useless to think without acting (as I did when the principal called me "girl" and I failed to protest).

Most of us don't need to think very long before we find ourselves guilty of one or the other of these harmful stances (acting without thinking, or thinking without acting). For example, it's likely that most teachers would say they believe that every human being—rich or poor, quick or slow—deserves to be treated with respect. (Certainly, I would have *said* that, even as I let male authorities treat me like a mindless child.) Like me, teachers who say they believe in human dignity and respect for others might find some distressing inconsistencies if they think carefully about their actual behaviors.

For example, you—you who are reading this paragraph—do you agree that, simply as human beings, students deserve to be treated with respect? OK, then here are some questions to think about. What kind of language do you use in your classroom and in the faculty lounge when you talk about students? Do you use disrespectful terms—morons, goofoffs, spoiled brats, bastards—to address or refer to your students? (An offensive term said jokingly is still an offensive term, and it signals that a socially acceptable form of humor is to demean whole groups of people.) Do you humiliate a student who transgresses some rule? Do you hand papers back in order of descending grades, so that students' right to privacy is violated? Do you give students a voice in your classroom? Do they have the right to ask questions, or are they silenced in your presence? Must they ask permission for taking care of personal matters, like trips to the bathroom or asking a neighbor for a tissue? If one of your colleagues is disrespectful to a student, what do you do about the behavior? If the principal implements a disrespectful punishment (the time my daughter's principal made her entire class kneel and press their noses to a wooden floor comes to mind), what do you do about it? A teacher who engages in speech or action disrespectful to students, or who fails to protest such behavior when others exhibit it, is not acting in a way consistent with a professed belief in respectful treatment of students.

It is the function of praxis to knit our thoughts and our actions together so that we develop a coherent way of living, in and out of our classrooms, in support of a particular vision of the way the world should be. I know that many readers will think "Hey, Pollyanna! You don't know my kids. They are animals." So let's stop here for a moment and examine the assumption underpinning that criticism. The implication is that some students are inherently wild, and must be reigned in as if they were horses. While it's true that students may act uncontrollably, there is more than one possible explanation for their behavior. Perhaps they are somehow inherently wild. But then again, maybe there are conditions that move them to refuse to be controlled by certain people in certain situations. Perhaps they are exhibiting resistance, for the very good reasons critical theorists believe they have identified. Trying to control students more and more and more is *one* action we might take in response to disruptive behavior. But another alternative, explored far too infrequently, is to think more deeply about *why* students may refuse to cooperate in schooling.

Educators interested in seriously rethinking the "control" issue might read Peter McLaren's text *Life in Schools*. No matter *how* unruly your students are, they're probably no worse than McLaren's, and this book offers enormous insight into what goes wrong in "bad" classrooms and schools; why things go wrong; and how teachers might act positively and effectively, instead of simply assuming the problem is *in* the kids. This text is listed in suggested readings at the end of this book, but I want to take special note of it here for teachers who have begun to suspect that being meaner and meaner might not be the best or only response—and who also agree with McLaren that it is unacceptable to continue simply throwing our hands up and writing off "uncontrollable" students.

BUT WHAT DOES THIS MEAN I SHOULD *DO* ?

If you want to improve the world—educational and otherwise— do anything and everything you can to move the world in the direction you'd like to see it go. Work on changing *anything* that you think needs to be changed.

Opportunities to develop critical consciousness and to formulate praxis abound for the classroom teacher. *Look* at the students in various tracks in your school: do all the children in the advanced or college prep groups have leather book bags, while all the children in the "slower" or vocational groups have shabby polyesters? If so, then you might start looking into how children are placed in your school, and whether those placements are reliably related to any factor besides social class. Do you teach science? Do your students know the names of female scientists as well as male ones? If not, why not? Do you watch to be sure that in labs, both sexes have equal opportunity to do hands-on work and to do the secretarial work? How much funding does your school allocate to boys' sports teams, how much to girls? Do you model democracy in your classroom by being open to dissent, by allowing students to help design classroom rules, by talking about going to the polls before or after school on election day?

Once we start thinking about everyday matters, it rapidly becomes obvious that *every*thing about schools and teacher behavior teaches students *some*thing by example. What do the students in your school learn from your behavior and school policies? Do they learn that how the world learn that everyone is entitled to fair and respectful treatment? Do they learn that sexes are equal, or that boys are better in math and science while girls are better at reading and writing? Do they learn that it's fine for a more powerful group to use a less powerful group for its own advantage, or do they learn that power is a resource that needs to be shared fairly? Do they learn to compete or to cooperate? Do they learn that adults lie, or that they honor integrity both by their actions and their words? Do they learn that to be a member of a community entails a responsibility to others who share that community, or do they learn that it's crazy to look out for anyone else? Do they learn that the appropriate response to anger is angry shouting, or do they learn about conflict resolution and compromise? In short, do you, your school, and the school staff and policies teach students that they are human beings who matter, or that they are dispensable annoyances? Do you teach them that they have to accept the world as it is, or do you teach them to think of themselves as change agents?

If you don't like some of your answers, then what can and will you do about it? Change your classroom practices? Speak with colleagues? Find new curricular materials? Ask to be on certain school committees? Pursue topics with administrators? Follow a topic through the chain of command, pursuing every channel to change things? Work for the school board candidates you believe in for the next school board election? Tell your union representatives that you don't like how they're representing you and you'll work to vote them out next time if things don't change? Try to form coalitions with like-minded colleagues, parents, administrators, staff?

What will you *do*?

Again, it's critical to remember that doing nothing *is* doing something. Doing nothing supports the status quo by allowing it to exist without challenge. Accepting the responsibility to formulate your own praxis is the alternative.

There is no way to avoid taking a stance.

A WORD ABOUT ATTITUDE: EMPOWERMENT

Once they understand that critical theory focuses on issues of power and disparity, many educators come to think of their task as *delivering* the disadvantaged from their conditions. This image of rescuer, however, badly misconstrues the critical educator's responsibility.

While a maiden locked in a tower may feel relieved to be released and carried off by a knight in shining armor, if he doesn't ask where *she* wants to go before carrying her off, or if he doesn't teach her how to avoid capture in the future, his help hasn't been worth very much. If he simply deposits her in his own castle, and if she must continue to depend on him, then all that he's done is transfer her dependence from the tyrant to himself. But she's still in a dependent state—and even a kind oppressor is still an oppressor.

Critical theorists do *not* try to *rescue* people from their lives. Instead, their goal is to equip others with the tools they need to deepen their understanding of their lives and to seek change *if* that is what they desire. The effective critical educator facilitates a process in which students learn to analyze their lives for themselves and to make their own, very conscious choices. To believe that a teacher knows better than students what choices are ultimately in their best interest is a form of cultural arrogance that critical educators shun. This provides an answer to an additional criticism of critical theory, that it does not offer a *specific* program for classroom educators to follow. However much practitioners might want theorists to give them one "right" set of practices, and however tempting that might be to those of us with a public voice and firm convictions, specific and universal recipes are neither possible nor morally acceptable. Every educator must design individual praxis for him or herself, as every human must decide for him or herself what kind of world she hopes to pursue.

Of course, the political agenda of critical theorists—to shift power and resources so that they are more equitably distributed—is no secret. But while they may frankly support that goal, that does *not* mean that they intend for their students to become flunkies in a new army. If students truly do develop critical consciousness and undertake praxis, then they are protected from unconsciously following anyone's agenda but their own. The very process is designed to negate the imposition of *any* form of constructed consciousness. None of the critical educators who have been my own mentors have told me what to do about sexism; they simply moved me to ask questions about why I buckled so easily to male authority and introduced me to praxis. The agenda I've designed——the drum that I currently march to—is entirely my own. And when a spokesperson for critical theory says something I don't like, I feel perfectly free to object. It is this sense of being able to do as I think best, after I've examined a topic from as many angles as I can access, that the critical theorist seeks to nurture in students.

The process, then, is not about rescue; it's about empowerment. When critical theorists talk about empowering their students, they are talking about helping them to attain mental freedom and to develop skills necessary to make their voices heard. Empowerment means helping others attain genuine power over their own choices and lives. The skills that they need to gain this power have important implications for curriculum and classroom practice.

TOOLS: CRITICAL ATTITUDES, CRITICAL LITERACIES

To free themselves from hegemonic ideas and take charge of their own choices, teachers must first develop the skepticism about the taken-for-granted that has been discussed in relation to critical consciousness. And, they must nurture that attitude in their students. An essential complement to this questioning is to cultivate a belief that things can indeed be other than they are, that the world can be shaped by individual and collective effort.

Deepening an understanding of how the world works, however, and of why things are as they are, requires a variety of critical literacies. Of course, people must become active and critical readers to hear what others are saying; in fact, much of what has been written about curricular implications focuses on the teaching of reading and writing. (Again, good sources are listed in the suggested readings.) Students must become skilled speakers and writers as well as readers so that they can have a voice in public conversations. But those skills are just the beginning.

To defend themselves against unconscious indoctrination, they must also develop media literacy. They must learn, for example, to analyze cultural messages in visual imagery—or in images that are avoided. What, for example, did the hugely popular Marlboro man suggest about the traits of a "man" in American society? Why was it a media event when the President of the United States chose to wear a sweater on television? Why haven't we seen a television show about life on a Native-American reservation? Why are so many women chained or nearly nude in rock videos?

To defend themselves from manipulation, students must also develop mathematical literacy. Knowing how to calculate an average is not enough. Americans have an enormous faith in numbers, and skilled rhetoricians use statistics frequently to manipulate public opinion. Having mathematical literacy includes such skills as being about to thoughtfully question reports involving numbers. Suppose, for example, a school boasted that 95% of students who graduated from its college preparatory program successfully completed college in four years. Someone needs to ask "Well, great, but in which colleges? And what percentage of your total high school population is *in* the college prep track? What is the average income of families those students come from? What percentage is in your vocational track? What is *their* mean family income? What percentage of students in your college prep track are African-American or Mexican-American or Native-American or Asian-American? What percentage of your total student body comes from those groups?"

To make this point about mathematical literacy in my own classroom I often show students a widely publicized report that listed SAT results in individual states along with the states' average teacher salaries. Because there was often little or no correlation between high SAT scores and high teacher salary (and sometimes an inverse relationship), the numbers were presented as if they proved that paying teachers more has little or no effect on student achievement (and so, they implied, there's no point in paying teachers big bucks). While this was a very popular message politically, it was anything but proven by the report. Several questions needed to be asked. For example, many of the lowest results clustered in the northeast United States, where there are large populations of students whose first language is not English and where students more frequently attend drastically underfunded urban schools. Moreover, the cost of living in such areas as New York tends to be higher than in the higher scoring middle states like Iowa, meaning that two teachers' salaries that *appear* widely disparate might be fairly equal in terms of buying power in their area. (How does rent in the New York City area compare, for example, with rents in rural Midwestern communities?) What is the effect of living in a tightly knit, traditional, two-parent, suburban community versus living in a highly fluid, urban area where many families are headed by a single female? Besides, *who* took the SATs, and what about people who didn't take them? And what exactly do the SATs measure, anyway? Is it a good measure of teachers' successes? Numbers never tell the whole story, and teachers and students alike must be empowered to question them.

Another necessary sort of literacy is political literacy. Everyone is part of multiple communities, and everyone has both the right and the responsibility to help shape those communities into places they're proud of. This means that everyone has the right and the responsibility to discover who exactly is making decisions that affect them and to think about how they might work to have some say in those decisions. For teachers, that means knowing who controls what in their schools, unions, and school districts, as well as on state and national levels. The seat of real power will vary, and teachers must learn either to work with who's in charge or else to help relocate the power. Instead of shunning involvement in activities outside the classroom, teachers need to volunteer for committees, go to meetings, be active politically, both locally and nationally.

Students must come to understand that they, too, are part of multiple communities, including their schools, neighborhoods, and nations. Like the teachers, they need to learn how to identify and address the powerful, to have a say in issues that concern them. They must learn that they, too, have a right and a responsibility to change things. In my children's highly rigid school, for example, where there is a lot of talk about the school "family," the female students started asking the reasonable questions "Why do we have to wear skirts and knee socks year round and suffer extreme cold in the winter? This is not healthful for us. What can we do to have this policy changed?" After speaking to several administrators, interested students found that the answer to the question of "Why do we have this policy?" fell under tradition: "Because that's what girls have *always* worn in this school." Deciding this wasn't good justification, a group of students approached administrators to request a change of policy. When it was denied, several wrote letters to the editor of the school newspaper. Then, they circulated a petition that was eventually presented to the administrators. When that accomplished nothing, many females started simply ignoring the dress code, wearing sweat pants under their skirts. That was tolerated for a few days, and then they started being sent to detention. A day or two of that, and most females were not only wearing sweats under their skirts, but *not* showing up for detention. And then, finally, the policy changed.

Nurturing empowerment among young people is not comfortable for parents and school authorities. Nurturing empowerment among teachers is not comfortable for administrators. Nurturing empowerment among citizens is not comfortable for politicians and power holders. But such empowerment is the heart of the democracy we promote so passionately in public speech. One other essential skill is implied in the above— research. Schools need to be places where everyone learns, and everyone knows how to learn. Everyone, in short, needs research skills, knowing how to find answers to such questions as "Who knows about this? What bias is there likely to be in information from this or that source? What written sources might be useful? Which people might it be useful to talk to? Who will be interested in what I find out? How can I share this information if I think it needs sharing?" And here we come full circle to critical reading and writing skills: schools must be places where people model and learn how to find information, sift through it, evaluate it, form it into coherent patterns, and be able to speak or write knowledgeably and persuasively about the resulting shape of their thinking. Voices on the pages of newspapers and journals need to include *teacher* voices much more often if teachers are to help define tomorrow's schools.

CURRICULAR IMPLICATIONS

There are no subject matter boundaries when it comes to equipping students with such tools. Students in every class can think critically and questioningly about what textbooks tell them, why that information has been included, and what's been left in and out of what they read. Students in every class can seek information outside the classroom and talk and write about it as part of classwork. Students preparing for a career in a trade can research the history of trade unions and ask questions about current conditions and what the responsibilities of union members and union representatives might be. Students studying science can learn how the sacred truth of one era turned into yesterday's myth in another era, and why so many inventions are credited to men. Any student can analyze why they have to take some subjects and not others, why they have so many or so few textbooks, why homes in their neighborhood are lushly landscaped or bullet-riddled, and what organization in their community they might join to support efforts to make their communities better. Students studying anything can monitor the media to see what's being said about that topic, how it's being said, and what effect the form of the message has on the information it contains. Questions and answers about how, why, so what, and what else is possible ought to be the natural stuff of every classroom. An emphasis on student questioning, research, and responsibility seems revolutionary *only* because a positivist agenda has been in place for so long.

Activism, too, should seem a natural part of classrooms. Young people have long proven their power. We've heard about students initiating recycling projects, projects to feed the homeless, and park rejuvenations. We need to stop perceiving such activities as *extra*ordinary and work to make them the natural product of our classroom teaching. Students should *become* change agents before they leave our schools, ready to aid in making their communities good places to live and work.

And, classrooms should teach what democracy is by example. As Freire writes in *A Pedagogy for Liberation*, "I cannot proclaim my liberating dream and in the next day be authoritarian in my relationship with the students." Student voices must be heard, their particular knowledge affirmed, and their concerns addressed. The teacher must be collaborator rather than oppressor. Any step toward a more democratic classroom moves a teacher's practice toward a critical pedagogy.

SO WHERE CAN I START?

No change is too small to make if it moves your practice closer to a vision you believe in. No goal is too unrealistic to pursue. Therefore, start anywhere. Or, if that advice seems overwhelming, start with questions like these:

1. Do I treat my students as if they are each valuable individuals, or as if they are subjects for me to control? To do well in my class, must students abandon their native speech and cultural habits? To what extent, if any, is my class about stuffing everyone into the same "American" mold?

2. Who has what kind of power in my own classroom? Why? Who gains what, who loses what, because of my power arrangement? How might it be otherwise? What would be gained, what lost, in other arrangements?

3. What classroom practice or school policy do I carry out even though I don't like or believe in it? Why? Who gains, who loses what? What purpose is it intended to serve? Does it accomplish its goal? Is that a goal I want to pursue? If so, how else might that be accomplished? What would be gained, what lost, in other alternatives? Whose cooperation would I need to make a change? How might I get it?

4. Does my class help students learn to question current conditions and assumptions? Does it teach them to be researchers, to develop the critical literacies they need to become change agents?

Where should you start? As the Kingsolver character says in the quote I mentioned earlier, the answer is "so simple I almost can't say it":

Start anywhere. Question anything. Question everything. Do what you think is *right* rather than what is expedient. And teach your students to do the same.

A Sketch of Further Reading[1]

Resources in Critical Theory

Kanpol, B. (1994). *Critical pedagogy: An introduction*. Westport, CT: Bergin & Garvey.

This book provides a logical next-step for readers who want more in the way of scholarship in the field, tied closely to practical classroom realities. Kanpol offers some scholarly depth in a wonderfully readable style. Full of classroom examples to make theory and pedagogy come alive, this is a text a novice can pick up with confidence—and is likely to put down with deeper understanding of important concepts and issues.

Kincheloe, J. & S. Steinberg, eds. (1992). *Thirteen questions: Reframing education's conversations*. New York: Peter Lang.

In this book, many of critical theory's most renowned spokespersons address such questions as "What are the basics and are we teaching them?" and "What are schools for and what should we be doing in the name of education?" Infinitely more accessible than *Breaking Free*, this text may still present a bit of a challenge for the novice who can't yet process terminology without frequently stopping to decode it. Still, the commentaries are provocative, and educators with a serious interest in the field ought to keep this book on their list of works to read at some point.

Leistyna, P., A. Woodrum, & S. Sherblom, eds. (1996). *Breaking free: The transformative power of critical pedagogy*. Cambridge: Harvard Educational Review.

Intended as an introduction to the field, this text features a collection of essays by prominent critical theorists, covering a wide range of issues. Despite the editors' introductions to the essays and a comprehensive glossary, readers not already comfortable with critical concepts may find the readings difficult. However, a wide-ranging annotated bibliography at the end of the text is a superb guide to further reading and easily makes the book worth its cost. Many books listed there are not listed here to avoid redundancy.

Wink, J. (1997). *Critical pedagogy: Notes from the real world.* New York: Longman.

A highly personal, highly readable, highly enlightening book about what critical theory and pedagogy have meant in the practice of one teacher. Wink is an engaging writer who introduces the reader to students and others we can learn from, and whose voice draws any reader into the ongoing conversation all critical educators engage in. Another great next-step for novices.

Understanding History, Hegemony and Oppression

Biklen, S. B. (1995). *School work: Gender and the cultural construction of teaching.* New York: Teachers College Press.

Scholarly and perhaps just a bit difficult to read, this book is well worth the effort. Biklen presents a thorough and interesting exploration of the impact of gender on the status of teaching. This text is likely to prove illuminating to anyone who has noted how reluctant teachers are to voice their opinions outside the faculty lounge, or how powerless they perceive themselves to be. Women especially are likely to find their experiences and attitudes affirmed and thoughtfully examined here, in an historical and cultural perspective.

Kozol, J. (1991). *Savage inequalities: Children in America's schools.*
New York: Crown.

Americans are taught that "In this country, anyone who works hard can be successful." Success is thought to be earned via hard work in school, where everyone has an equal chance to learn. Kozol debunks this myth of American schooling by a fact-filled and very tough look at conditions in cities nationwide, where different schools in the same district offer students anything *but* an equal education. Readers will meet underprivileged children who lack teachers, facilities, equipment and respect, but who are all too familiar with tragedy. In fact, any citizen of the United States who believes in real democracy and social justice needs to read this book—and pass it around.

Loewen, J. (1995). *Lies my teacher told me: Everything your American history textbook got wrong.* New York: The New Press.

It's extremely difficult to imagine and realize critical practice without first understanding in some depth how schools serve decidedly political agendas. By detailing omissions and inaccuracies prevalent in history textbooks, Loewen makes clear how they manipulate student perceptions and how schooling subsequently serves to maintain certain hegemonies. An easy-to-read and eye-opening text for anyone.

Spring, J. (1994). *Deculturalization and the struggle for equality: A brief history of the education of dominated cultures in the United States.* New York: McGraw-Hill.

Spring's text documents how schools have been used to oppress groups whose land or cheap labor was valued by mainstream America. This is a short text packed full of facts that go far to explain why American schools too often fail with today's Native American, Puerto Rican and Mexican

American students. Anyone who doesn't know that Native American children were once removed to boarding schools and forbidden to speak their native language, or who don't know that Cherokee schools once produced a near 100% literacy rate (far above the rates of Texas or Arkansas at the time) will find interesting food for thought here.

Literacy and Critical Theory

Knoblauch, C. H. and L. Brannon. (1993). *Critical teaching and the idea of literacy.* Portsmouth, NH: Boynton Cook.

These authors are nearly peerless in knitting together the subtleties of theory with daily realities of the classroom and cultural climate. In this text, they explore the role of language in shaping the schools we've inherited and the politics surrounding—and impeding—genuine classroom reform. They provide real insight into how politics is shaping contemporary debates and real information to counter attacks on reform.

Shannon, P., ed. (1992). *Becoming political: Readings and writings in the politics of literacy education.* Portsmouth, NH: Heinemann.

Literacy is a recurring concern of political theorists, for reasons which become clear in this collection of essays about various facets of literacy instruction. This is a text that can be browsed through, can be picked up and put down at will, and can be shared with others. An especially good choice for elementary school teachers and other teachers of reading and writing.

Smith, F. (1986). *Insult to intelligence.* Porstmouth, NH: Heinemann.

While this is not an obviously critical text, Smith does an excellent job of demonstrating how positivist assumptions and procedures function to disempower teachers and students. Written for a lay audience and specifically about reading instruction, this important book is easily accessible to any reader and offers powerful ammunition for waging war against dehumanizing school practices. Another must on anyone's education book shelf.

Note

1. The word "sketch" for the title of this section was deliberate. This is by no means an exhaustive, or even reasonably inclusive, bibliography. Again, as I did above, I refer the reader to the extensive annotated bibliography in *Breaking Free* for a wider selection of materials. My intention here has been only to be sure that an interested reader has at least some idea of where he or she might turn next. Alternatives to these suggestions are innumerable.

References

Ayers, W. (1993). *To teach.* New York: Teachers College Press.

Bambara, T. C. (1972). The lesson. In D. Hunt (ed.), *The Riverside anthology of literature.* 1988. Boston: Houghton Mifflin.

Berry, W. (1988). "People, land, and community." In R. Simonson & W. Walker (eds.), The Graywolf annual five: Multicultural literacy. Saint Paul, MN: Graywolf Press.

Cherryholmes, C. (1988). *Power and criticism: Poststructural investigations in education.* New York: Teachers College Press.

Coyle, M. (1992). *The New Jersey High School Proficiency Test in Writing: A pragmatic face on an autonomous model.* Unpublished doctoral dissertation. Teachers College, Columbia University.

Crane, S. (1968) *Maggie: A girl of the streets,* 1893 edition. Boston: D. C. Heath.

Dewey, J. (1938). *Experience and education.* New York: Collier.

Freire, P. (1970). *Pedagogy of the oppressed.* New York: Continuum.

Freire, P. (1973). *Education for critical consciousness.* New York: Continuum.

Freire, P. (1978). *Pedagogy-in-process.* New York: Continuum.

Freire, P. (1985). *The politics of education.* South Hadley, MA: Bergin & Garvey.

Freire, P. & Faundez, A. (1992). *Learning to question: A pedagogy of liberation.* New York: Continuum.

Frost, R. (1969). "Mending wall" In E. Lathem (ed.), *The Poetry of Robert Frost.* New York: Henry Holt & Co.

166

Gordimer, N. (1981). *July's people*. New York: The Viking Press.

Heath, S. B. (1983). *Ways with words: Language, life and work in communities and classrooms*. New York: Cambridge University Press.

Herrnstein, R. (1994). *The Bell Curve: Intelligence and class structure in American life*. New York: Free Press.

Hostile hallways: The AAUW survey on sexual harassment in America's schools. (1993). Washington, D.C.: AAUW Educational Foundation.

Johnson, L. (1983). "For my Indian daughter. In K. Flachmann & M. Flachmann (eds.), *The prose reader: Essays for thinking, reading, and writing*. Englewood Cliffs, NJ: Prentice Hall.

Kingsolver, B. (1990). *Animal dreams*. New York: HarperCollins.

Knoblauch, C. & Brannon, L. (1993). *Critical teaching and the idea of literacy*. Portsmouth, NH: Heinemann.

Kozol, J. (1991). *Savage inequalities: Children in America's schools*. New York: Crown.

Lame Deer & Erdoes, R. (1993). From Lame Deer: Seeker of Vision. In P. Riley (ed.), *Growing up Native American: An anthology*.

Listening to America with Bill Moyers: Unequal education. (1992). Videotape. Alexandria, VA: PBS Video.

Mayher, J. (1990). *Uncommon sense: theoretical practice in language education*. Portsmouth, NH: Heinemann.

McLaren, P. (1989). *Life in schools*. New York: Longman.

Morrison, T. (1972). *The bluest eye*. New York: Simon & Schuster.

Owen, D. (1987). Math discovery. In *Plain talk about learning and writing across the curriculum*. VA: Virginia Department of Education.

Rosenblatt, L. (1983). *Literature as exploration*. New York: Modern Language Association. (Originally published in 1938)

Sadker, M. & Sadker, D. (1994). *Failing at fairness: How America's schools cheat girls*. New York: Scribner's.

Shortchanging girls, shortchanging America. (1991). Washington, D.C.: AAUW.

Sizer, T. (1984). *Horace's compromise: The dilemma of the American high school*. Boston, MA: Houghton Mifflin.

Smith, F. (1986). *Insult to intelligence: The bureaucratic invasion of our classrooms*. Portsmouth, NH: Heinemann.

Spring, J. (1996). *American education*. New York: McGraw-Hill.

Tan, A. (1995). *The hundred secret senses*. New York: G. P. Putnam's Sons.

Tannen, D. (1986). *That's not what I meant*. New York: Morrow.

Walker, A. (1979). We alone. *Horses make a landscape look more beautiful*. New York: Harcourt Brace Jovanovich.

Index